No Time to Grow?

Gardening Solutions for a Busy Life.

By Tim Wootton

ISBN 978 1 90487 148 4
A catalogue record for this book is available from
the British Library.

Published by
The Good Life Press Ltd.
PO Box 536
Preston
PR2 9ZY

www.goodlifepress.co.uk
www.homefarmer.co.uk

Set by The Good Life Press Ltd.

Printed and bound in Great Britain by
CPI Antony Rowe, Chippenham and Eastbourne

No Time to Grow?

Gardening Solutions for a Busy Life

By Tim Wootton

The Good Life Press LTD

Contents

No Time to Grow?

This book is for everyone who cares about the food they eat, would like to produce as much of it as possible but is intimidated by the time pressures of modern life. It is aimed at all of us whose lives are too busy to spend the time we would like in the garden, but who refuse to give in entirely to the pressure to conform and to buy everything through the commercial system. The philosophy is always that it is better to produce something than to not try and hence to produce nothing. The book sets out to demonstrate ways of working and of thinking to enable the production of a relatively large amount of fruit and vegetables with a minimal time investment.

Why Grow It Yourself Anyway?

The fact is that if you've gone to the trouble of buying this book you probably already have your own answer to this question. However, if by chance you're still browsing through it or have been given it by some misguided friend or relative, then here are some of the reasons you might like to consider, or at least here are some of my reasons for doing so.

My own main motivation is simply a desire to take control of this one important aspect of my life. There are so many areas of our modern lives which are dominated by large organisations and over which we have little control. I don't like the idea of my entire diet falling into the same category. It is true that there is a great deal of good quality food available, but I don't want to constantly have to rely on someone else to produce it and on someone else's word that it has been produced to the highest standards. There is something fundamental about producing one's own food, something which links us with our past and our ancestors. It gives a feeling of satisfaction and a self-reliance that endures the knocks of life. True, it's good to know that our food has been produced without damaging the environment in its production and has only required minimal transportation, but the reasons I grow it are more fundamental than these.

Since I started writing this book the twin issues of climate change and peak oil have come very much to the fore. It is clear that in the near future our society will, as a whole, become more dependant on local resilience rather than the international supply chains which, in the recent past, have dictated our needs and requirements. There are many other good books that examine the wider implications of, and our responses to, this new reality, but I hope some of my suggestions on food production may assist busy modern people in their quest for a more independent lifestyle.

Some General Principles

Before outlining a specific plan I'd like to set out some general principles which underlie my thinking and which govern what I hope to achieve.

Keep it Simple

In other words, don't attempt to produce too many different crops too soon. The bigger the range of crops attempted, the bigger the range of conflicting requirements and the more demands on your time. Better to grow a smaller range well than to have a long list of heroic failures. Doubling the quantity of one crop is usually easier and less work than using the same area for two different crops, but there is obviously only any point in doing so if all the produce can be used.

Work with Nature, not Against It

I grow organically and have written everything in this book on that basis. Personally I can see very little point in going to the trouble of producing my own food only to risk contamination from chemical residues and so produce something that is no better than most commercially produced food. Similarly, I gain a great deal of pleasure from the natural world in which I garden and can't conceive of risking damaging it just to produce a little more.

To reduce work I also extend this principle to growing crops when they want to grow. For example, why waste effort cosseting cucurbits in April when they could simply be sown and planted out later. The delay to harvest times is usually minimal as plants grown under their preferred conditions usually catch up. Even if they don't, a slightly later or smaller harvest achieved without much work is better than a complete failure due to over ambition and insufficient time to complete the job.

Select Crops to Avoid Problems

If you are unlikely to have time to pick a crop every couple of days to prevent it going over, concentrate on less fussy crops that can be harvested when it suits you. In my basic plan I grow French beans for drying which can be harvested in a single go, rather than green or runner beans which spoil if they aren't picked every 2-3 days. The emphasis has to be on planning out problems rather than taking action when they arise. In the longer term this reduces the time required for successful gardening, more than any other single factor.

Carrots Aren't just Carrots…etc.

Contrary to the impression we get in most supermarkets, all major fruit and vegetable crops are available to the grower in a multitude of varieties. Each of these varieties has been created by selection, at some time in the past, for a particular set of characteristics. Inevitably, the majority of varieties have been developed for the benefit of the commercial system (e.g. those which can be harvested in one go and can sit on the supermarket shelf for ages without appearing to deteriorate) but a growing minority offer the characteristics we are looking for, to reduce our work without sacrificing quality. Disease and pest resistance are key properties to look for as it means less time is occupied combating problems. Even if you don't plan to grow organically it's worth picking varieties described as 'suitable for organic cultivation' for this reason. Also, in most cases, plants with a long cropping season usually make sense as less will be wasted if the harvesting is a bit erratic. Overall, time spent going through the seed and plant catalogues before the growing season begins is a very good investment at a time of year when things are slack in the garden.

Be Honest with Yourself

If there's no way you've got time to achieve something, change the plan and do something else, or grow something different. Challenges and experimentation are obviously good ideas, but to continue an earlier example, if all we end up with is a mountain of inedible, stringy runner beans we are not going to be very pleased with our efforts, and will struggle to motivate ourselves in future. Make sure any experiments really are experiments: keep them small until the concept is proven and learn from both positive and negative results.

Be Organised

Work through the plan in detail, mentally at least. When short of time don't use the vital weekly hour on the vegetable patch for basic planning activities. Instead, use other less productive moments for this planning. Since it is largely a mental activity, a lunch break on a working day, time while travelling or other unproductive parts of your week can all be utilised for this purpose. Incidentally, much of this book was planned while travelling on unrelated business. Remember that good planning will save time and prevent the majority of disappointments.

Be Patient

The Basic Plan, central to the theme of this book, can be achieved in less than an hour per week and maintained in even less. However, it will take (calendar) time to get there. This low level of time investment cannot possibly achieve results at the speed of a television-style garden makeover.

Keep the Soil in Use

Once the ground has been cleared the grower needs to maintain control over it. The easiest way of doing this is to keep crops in the ground for as much of the time as possible. When this is not possible the combination of black plastic covers and green manure crops (see Sustaining the Plan) will either prevent weed growth or out-compete them. Remember that nature abhors a vacuum and that an empty space will always end up being filled with something (in this case, weeds), the removal of which will create extra work for the gardener. If there's no space there will be fewer weeds and less work. A lot of space in this book is given to taking control of the land since failure to do so, and failure to maintain that control, is what causes hard-pressed gardeners to waste much of their valuable time, so be aware of this fact and plan accordingly.

Plant Out And Sow When There Is A Good Chance Of Success

Given that generally we haven't got time for either lots of watering or to erect and maintain complex plant protection measures, we must look to sow seed and plant out seedlings when they have a good chance of success without our intervention. For example, I won't plant out autumn/winter brassicas in the middle of a mid-summer drought. If I don't expect to be able to look after them, I simply wait until the weather appears to have broken (not a long wait in English summers!). A smaller or later crop is better than none at all. Obviously, there are no absolute guarantees and the weather fools us all, including the forecasters, from time to time, but I think this is the only option for those of us short of time.

Sow & Plant Throughout the Year

Many traditional gardeners will do nearly all their planting and sowing between March and May and have very little in the ground (perhaps a few spring brassicas and some leeks) over winter. This won't work for us. There is never enough time in the spring to start off everything I'd like to grow. It also tends to waste good growing conditions during the autumn, spring and also during unpredictable winter mild spells. It is much better to have a succession of crops going in at different times of year. This not only helps to spread the workload but also uses the ground efficiently. Remember also that any empty ground will fill up with weeds more quickly than ground in use, creating further jobs to occupy our time. So, by having a succession of crops at different times of the year, you are simply taking and maintaining control of the land with a minimum of effort and time and producing more!

- 11 -

How Much Land ?

Don't take on more land than you really have time to use. I've made this mistake in the past. It results in spending most of your time fighting weeds rather than producing anything useful, which is both dispiriting and discouraging. Try to make maximum use of the land at your disposal before expanding. If you have more land than you can use right now, keep it covered with a non-degrading mulch (e.g. black plastic sheeting) so that it will be weed free when you come to use it. Alternatively, green manure crops can be sown on land temporarily out of production to protect and raise fertility for its return to use.

Grow What You Eat Or Eat What You Grow?

There is clearly no point in producing food that your family will not eat; only a fool would think otherwise. However, our ability to produce our own food from scratch coupled with our concerns about commercial production and the carbon footprint created by worldwide distribution systems, should start to challenge elements of our diet. Over a period of time perhaps we should be looking for ways in which to produce new crops to replace some of the imported and most environmentally dubious foodstuffs. As the world economy changes with ever rising fuel prices, the option of importing most of our food will become a thing of the past and we may all have to become self-reliant once again.

Chapter One
Getting the Land into Production

When you first get hold of your plot of land it is reasonable to assume that it will be at least moderately overgrown with weeds and other undesirable species. If there's only a covering of this year's annual weeds you should think yourself lucky and anything less is a real bonus. The issue then is how to get it into cultivation. I have been presented with allotment plots that are closer to rough meadows than market gardens. They have comprised thick, tussocky grasses interspersed with dandelions and docks and riddled throughout with a network of bindweed, not to mention the rubbish to remove. The temptation is to reach for a powerful weed-killer on the dubious premise that 'just one hit to get started can't do too much harm; I'll go for organic solutions from then on'. Personally, this has never been a route I've been prepared to go down. I tend to think that one's land is either free of pesticides or it isn't and at least I know that if the land is this badly infested with weeds it can't have seen weed killer for a good few years. Why spoil that good record just before starting to garden? Also, on a bad plot it's very easy to let that just one hit with the herbicide extend to 'just until it's clear', and then perhaps to 'just to stop infringement at the edges', and then perhaps…. and so it goes on until it becomes the chosen method of operating.

In view of time limitations I tend to work in a gradual way, taking and maintaining control of the ground section by section. It is clearly vital to keep control of an area once the battle for clearance has been won and hence prevent the return of the jungle. This may be by carefully selective cropping or by keeping the ground covered.

On taking on a new, heavily overgrown plot during the growing season my first action is to, as far as possible, remove the heads of any weeds that have obviously set seeds. It's also a good idea to remove any brambles, seedling/sapling trees, or any other woody species – I use a combination of secateurs and a mattock. This material, together with the seed heads, is best burnt as soon as it is dry enough. After this, cut down all the remaining vegetation as close to the ground as possible using shears, sickle, scythe or even a petrol-driven strimmer or bush-cutter. There is no need to remove any of this material from where it falls. Now cover as much of the area as possible with black plastic and weigh down the edges with heavy objects or bury it in the ground. The plants trapped under the plastic are now deprived of any light and will slowly die and decompose.

It may make sense to deliberately exclude a small area from the plastic treatment. This needs to be small enough to clear thoroughly by hand in time to get a quick crop in before the growing season ends. Some short season potatoes (known as earlies) would be ideal if you can save some until the ground is ready for them. It's a good feeling to get a crop, no matter how small, from a corner of your new plot while you do battle with the rest of it.

I would leave the plastic on until late the following winter or even early spring. By this time most of the ordinary grasses will be dead and largely decomposed. Also, the ground should be reasonably dry and easy to dig, since all the autumn or winter rains will have run off. Now dig over as much of this ground as you have time for. At this stage the bulk of the bindweed roots will still be present (and probably ground elder too, if you are unfortunate enough to have this species), but only fragments of the other weed roots will remain. The workable soil and the destruction of the thick thatch will make these reasonably easy to remove. However, the removal of every last scrap of these perennial weeds has always proved impossible for me, and so some straggling tendrils will always appear during the first crops on any newly cleared ground. I would therefore just clear enough ground to grow a large crop of potatoes, preferably second earlies. I plant these in shallow trenches in early April. Creating the trenches gives me an extra chance to pick over the ground for root fragments. I also scrape out tendrils as they appear between the rows of potatoes in May, but weed growth is limited once the canopy of potatoes covers the ground. Then, in July and August as the potatoes are harvested, the remaining bindweed plants can be lifted at the same time, leaving the ground more or less clear for more sensitive future crops.

This approach not only clears the ground, but usually gives an excellent quick crop of potatoes too. I use second earlies for this purpose as first earlies don't always give enough of a canopy to cut out the light and minimise weed growth, and main crop potatoes can be in the ground too long: I don't especially want to have to separate bindweed fragments from wet autumn soil. I've also amazed my allotment neighbour with a higher yield from my new but very rough patch than he got from his pristine, lovingly manured one. The point he forgets is that my soil contained all the humus produced by many years of grasses and other deep-rooted weeds. Virtually none of the nutrients had been lost and were therefore available for the benefit of the crop. I didn't have to manure the ground because there was no need, so yet again saved time and effort.

Returning to the clearance of the plot, I suggested only bothering to clear part of the land in this way. If part of the land can be left underneath the plastic for the entire second season, the remaining weeds should die as well, making the final digging and clearance of the site a simple matter. Alternatively, if you didn't manage to get the plastic over most of the plot in the first season, it can be moved onto the untouched land and the process begun again. Decisions on how to manage things usually come down to how much time can be invested. If the whole plot has been covered in black plastic in the first summer, as described, the spring and summer of the second season can be spent slowly digging over the ground, gradually rolling back the plastic all the time, with the potatoes growing away on about a third of the land. It is important, though, to make use of the land once it has been cleared, as weed growth will rapidly resume.

If a useful further section can be cleared by mid-May it's worth having a transplant crop (e.g. sweetcorn, squashes, French beans) ready to go in. A direct sown crop is likely to be swamped by weed seedlings and residual bindweed. I've suggested these three crops because they can all be cleared in early autumn and the ground dug again to get out the last fragments of the perennial weeds. Leeks or winter brassicas could be used, but I would rather use a crop that gave me the chance to make another onslaught on the weed root system before next winter. If there isn't time to get a worthwhile crop in on the last section of ground to be dug, then consider the use of a green manure crop (see Sustaining the Plan - Chapter 3), or simply roll the black plastic back over the bare ground and wait until the following spring. Working this way nutrients are preserved and the ground remains free of weeds until it's needed. Leaving it open just creates more work for the future.

Some gardeners actually recommend cutting holes in plastic ground cover and planting through it, in order to get a crop while the clearing process is underway. I've not found this to be very effective, although I assume it must work in some circumstances. One year I ruined a large plastic sheet by cutting planting slits for courgettes and planted them out, only to get the entire crop eaten by slugs. The decaying vegetation, protected by a plastic sheet, provided a haven for the slugs and snails. If you are fortunate not to have such a thriving mollusc population, the technique may well work for you, but as an organic grower working on heavy, usually infested, soil I shan't try it again. As a general point, I've found that the slug population of newly cleared ground is usually very high, but it's pretty much impossible to do much about it until the ground is clear. After this, manual removal and beer traps will serve to reduce the level to more manageable proportions. However, it's still best to grow only tubers and transplanted crops in the first few years, as tiny seedlings are so easily decimated. Slug killing nematodes are another good but slightly pricy option, but even these can't be applied until the ground is clear.

Until recently organic gardeners were keen on using old carpet as a free alternative to black plastic when clearing the ground. In the short term it proves a very effective method, but in the longer term concerns have been raised over the tendency of some carpets to decay and to release unpleasant chemicals into the soil as they do so. Some allotment holders were guilty of leaving the carpets down for years on end. I don't have a major worry about using carpets briefly (i.e. up to one season), especially if they are my own and I know what's been used to clean them. However, shifting a large area of sodden carpet at the end of that time can in itself be a major struggle!

Chapter Two
The Basic Plan

This chapter describes in some detail how an overgrown plot can be brought into full production over a period of a couple of years, with the commitment of only around an hour's effort per week. I don't claim it to be the only possible plan, but it is here to provide one detailed example of how a totally unmanaged plot can be restored with only a modest investment of time. It is a tried and tested model, which can be adapted to suite individual needs and preferences. The time-scale of only achieving full production on each of 3 large beds by the third growing season may appear very slow, but it is the result of a staged build up, giving some production in years one and two. If a little more time can be found for preparation during the winter months, then all three beds could quite easily be in production in year two. The selection of crops used in this Basic Plan was made for ease of production, to guarantee control over the ground with minimal effort. Once this has been achieved changes can be wrung and a bigger variety or more exciting crops grown, as discussed in later chapters.

The land in question is based around a modest allotment plot on the grounds that this probably represents the hardest possible situation for the new grower to achieve success. Anything that is suggested here can more easily be achieved in a domestic garden, if you are fortunate enough to have a reasonable size growing plot at home. Techniques proposed for converting field grasses into vegetable beds will clearly also work on lawns!

The Plot

The plot where I developed this method measured around 8 metres by 10, and had a thick bramble hedge along one side (to the East). It was heavily overgrown, being more a bit of rough meadow than a garden.

I decided to put a shed into the North East corner next to the hedge to minimise the effect of the shade cast, and to leave the remaining areas along the hedge as the last to be cultivated, as the presence of the hedge would tend to make this the poorest growing area. I then divided the land to the West of the shed into 3 identical beds separated by 2 narrow, fixed paths, as shown in the diagram below.

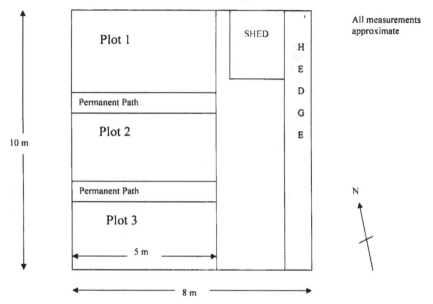

As I took on this severely overgrown plot in mid-summer I didn't attempt to get much in the way of crops underway during that first summer. I started by cutting down grasses and other weeds to prevent their seeding and removed what self-sown saplings and bramble roots there were as described in the previous chapter. The only attempt at cropping that summer was a small row of potatoes put into a still extremely weedy Bed 3. I do like to have at least something to show for the season's efforts, although in this case the crop was light and rather slug infested. With hindsight I probably planted the wrong variety.

After cutting down the tall grasses and other weeds, I put down a large sheet of black polythene. I bought a piece big enough to cover the whole of Bed 1 and part of Bed 2 in a single sheet. I find builders' merchants are the best supplier of this invaluable product as they usually stock a heavy duty version from a roll which, when fully opened out, expands to cover a 4 metre width. This has the flexibility of enabling me to buy whatever length I need in a large width. It can be rather expensive but will last for at least 4 or 5 years and does a much better job than the narrower strips which need to be overlapped to complete the coverage.

This large area (about 20m²) of plastic was weighted down and dug in securely at the edges. The whole patch was then left until the following January, except for harvesting the small potato crop from Bed 3 in the autumn.

By New Year the vast majority of the weeds under the black plastic had rotted. It was necessary to dig through the soil carefully to sift out the remaining persistent bindweed and couch grass roots, but the dense thatch of other grasses had all but decomposed. This dig also served to incorporate the remaining largely composted plant material into the soil. Because the ground had been protected from the rain since July my heavy clay based soil remained friable (easily crumbled) and easy to dig. As I cleared Bed 1 during the next few weeks I gradually rolled back the plastic to expose the soil to the elements. This enabled rain-water to be absorbed and also removed the protection from the numerous slugs and snails sheltering underneath.

By late March Bed 1 was completely clear and ready for its first crop. I planted 3, 5 metre rows of a potato called Kestrel. This is a particularly useful potato as it grows quickly to smother out the inevitable carpet of annual weeds found in such new ground. It is a second early, giving a good yield by July or August and is therefore generally out of the way when potato blight strikes. It is also largely resistant to slugs, making it ideal for use in new ground. Fortunately I find this particular variety far more appetising than the slugs do!

Having got the first crop underway I was able to move the plastic sheet across so that the remainder of Bed 2 was covered, plus a good part of Bed 3. More digging and weed root removal during March and April enabled me to have a good half of Bed 2 completely clear by early May and the plastic sheet moved across to completely cover Bed 3. At this point I suspended my ground clearance activities, leaving the last bit of

Bed 2 and the whole of Bed 3 to their own devices under the plastic for the whole of the growing season ahead.

In early April I'd raised some sweetcorn plants from seed using root trainers, first located on a warm windowsill and then hardened off on a patio table. These were planted out in 2 rows each of 15 plants, using slightly more than half of Bed 2. Sweetcorn is an easy crop to grow but is susceptible to cold winds and frost early in the season. It is possible to provide protection from adverse weather but this is an extra, time consuming, task. My answer is therefore to simply delay its planting out until the weather has really warmed up. Living in the West Country I find that it is generally safe to plant out such crops by around the second week in May, depending on conditions at the time. Further North delaying slightly longer would probably be wise. The thinking here is that it is better to wait until the conditions are right and, if necessary, put the date of harvest back a bit, than it is to risk the crop or commit to extra tasks for which the time may not be available. Besides, strongly growing plants put out in good conditions will usually catch up anything planted out too early in cold weather.

Having put in the first real season's crops there was little to do other than maintaining the plot and preventing regression to its former overgrown state, at least for the next few months. I find that a regular hoeing between plants and along paths is the quickest way of keeping the weeds in check. At this stage, as little as 10 minutes per week was sufficient to maintain control and to start depleting the weed seed bank in the soil. I prefer to use a light-weight hoe with a small head and a pull-push action, as I find this type of implement is easiest to get between closely growing plants. It was also necessary to give the remaining untouched areas a going over to prevent weeds setting seeds and generally getting out of hand. As the area remaining uncultivated or uncovered is now fairly small (under 20m²), I used a sickle to keep it under control. This created a generous supply of green material and so I added a compost bin to capture this free supply of future soil enrichment.

The potatoes were harvested over a six-week period from early July to mid-August. They provided a good harvest (around 65kg) which stored quite well, keeping my family of 5 in potatoes from the first harvest in July until late November. The sweetcorn too did reasonably, averaging around one cob per plant and was harvested from late August to mid-September.

In September, once Bed 1 was clear of potatoes, the ground was given a quick forking over to remove the inevitable residual weed roots and the crop was replaced by onion sets. Two varieties of over-wintering onion sets, one red and one white, were selected and a series of short rows were planted covering most of Bed 1. From my experience it's important to get this crop in reasonably early to ensure that the plants are well established before winter sets in. Later in the autumn a couple of rows of garlic cloves were added to the now expanding allium bed in Bed 1. The sweetcorn plants in Bed 2 were cleared and the bed dug over during the autumn, but no further planting was carried out here.

The following winter followed much the same pattern, except that it was Bed 3 and the final part of Bed 2 rather than Bed 1 that received the thorough digging over. The alliums in Bed 1 were more or less left to their own devices, with just the occasional hoeing as weeds sprouted in milder periods. Again, the one hour time allowance was sufficient to complete the digging of Bed 2 by March and Bed 3 by April.

In this second full growing season Bed 2 became the potato bed (Kestrel again) and the sweetcorn went into Bed 3. I felt that the half bed of sweetcorn grown the previous season had been sufficient so, rather than expand this crop to fill the space available, I filled the remainder of Bed 3 with a combination of climbing French beans (grown for dried beans) and pumpkins. These crops were chosen for their ease of production and similar seasons. All could be planted out in mid-May and all would be cleared by early October, if not before. With this more demanding planting regime more time was needed this season away from the bed producing the seedlings, but since the clearance and digging activities were complete by April, the spring sowing and potting on seedlings didn't present too great an overall burden. In total 21 climbing French bean plants (3 rows of 7), 24 sweetcorn (3 x 8) and 3 pumpkin plants were planted out, although a few spares of each were produced in case of mishap. The choice of beans for drying was made on the grounds that this is another 'plant and forget 'til harvest' crop. Beans for eating green are very good to eat and just as easy to produce, but they need picking every couple of days, which doesn't suit the hour-a-week grower.

This year fewer over-wintering onions were grown, but the remaining space in Bed 1 was filled with spring-planted onion sets and a few shallots. These were planted in March with a view to an August harvest, thus spreading the onion harvest over a couple of months.

The summer plot maintenance activities were kept to a minimum. All the transplants were watered well when put in, but received very little watering after that. Weeding was done almost entirely with the hoe and, although both Beds 1 and 3 needed weekly attention, this could still be achieved in about 15 minutes. The only feeding of the plants was a scattering of pelleted chicken manure applied to the over wintering onions in late March and to the beans and corn etc. in June.

The harvest during this second season was spread from mid-June when the first of the over-wintered onions became usable, through the potato harvest in July and August, sweetcorn in early September and beans and pumpkins in late September to mid-October. Importantly though, since none of the crops were too sensitive to harvest times, they could all be brought in at a point to suit my timetable rather than demanding my attention every few days for weeks on end, as some more fussy crops are inclined to do.

After this harvest the 3-bed cycle is complete and all that now remains is to rotate the crops through the beds. Before this second season is complete the over-wintering onions will go into Bed 2 after the potatoes and next spring the next potato crop will go into Bed 3 with the sweetcorn, beans and pumpkins together in Bed 1.

Having got the whole area into production the winter digging load becomes much lighter. Each summer the former potato bed needs to be forked over and levelled before the onions are put in, but the other two beds still need to be turned over each winter. In my experience it will take many years before a really heavily infested plot will be totally fee of perennial weeds, and the winter digging is of primary importance in keeping bindweed and other such crop-choking species under control. To ease the load in getting through this digging I would still recommend covering at least one of the two beds to be dug with the plastic sheet during the first half of the winter. This will weaken weeds, if not kill all of them outright, and also keep the soil light and diggable when the task has to be carried out in January and February. It also makes it possible to get in your weekly hour's digging on the allotment when all around is frozen solid!

Rotation Summary

The crops and activities described in creating this particular low effort model can be summarised as follows:

Bed \ Year	Year 1	Year 2	Year 3
Bed 1	Potatoes	Alliums	Sweetcorn, drying beans, pumpkins
Bed 2	Sweetcorn – half bed only	Potatoes	Alliums
Bed 3	Unused – under plastic	Sweetcorn, drying beans, pumpkins	Potatoes

After the above cycle has been completed the fourth season could simply be a repetition of the first, but with all 3 Beds fully utilised. However, with the system now running smoothly and the ground largely under control, more can be attempted.

Although the rotation has worked well for the first few years it cannot be expected to do so ad infinitum, unless serious steps are taken to maintain the fertility of the soil. We cannot expect to continuously take from the soil without putting anything back. Furthermore, to use a 3 year rotation indefinitely would be taking a definite risk. Over time species specific pests and diseases can build up in the soil and specific nutrients and trace elements will be removed. These effects can be minimised by practicing good crop rotation, but the minimum period for such a rotation is usually regarded as 4 years. The short rotation of the Basic Plan is a good start, but needs further development to be sustainable over the longer term. These issues are covered in the next couple of chapters.

One note to add: after using this plan for several seasons on my allotment in rural Somerset, I've given up on growing sweetcorn as part of the third item in the rotation, although the beans and pumpkins remain. After my first successful year with sweetcorn in the plan, it has been discovered by both the local deer and badgers, who both make special trips to the allotments to eat this crop. They flatten the plants and leave nothing edible behind. One day I may get round to building a strong fence around the plot, but until then sweetcorn is definitely off the plan. Hopefully those who live in more urban locations won't be troubled by these particular pests.

Chapter Three
Sustaining the Plan

One of the best things about taking on a new, heavily overgrown patch of land is that the fertility of the soil is likely to be high. Generations of grasses and other plants will have grown on the site and will now be at various stages of decomposition in the surface layer of the soil. The methods of preparing the land described earlier have been designed to make maximum use of this ready supply of nutrients. As growers we therefore only have to think in terms of maintaining fertility, rather than creating it in the first place. It is usually reasonable to assume that if the soil can support a rich 'crop' of weeds, it will also support a good initial vegetable crop. In fact the 3 years of cropping described in the Basic Plan could, when I tried it, be supported with only a few minor additions to this initial nutrient bank. However, it would be foolish to continue cropping for much longer without taking steps to replace the nutrients removed from the soil.

If, at the start of the project, the newly acquired land appeared to be having difficulty in growing weeds there would have been real cause for concern. This is only really likely to occur on light, sandy soils where it may be necessary to consider giving new land a fertility boost from the start. But at least in these circumstances clearing the land won't be the demanding task it proves to be on rich, heavy soils.

As an organic grower I would insist that the only acceptable way of raising the long term fertility of the soil is by incorporating a large volume of organic material which will decay slowly, releasing plant nutrients as it does so. This is true whether it is done before the land is used for the first time or after a few crops have been grown and fertility starts falling. Small scale additions can be made as quick fixes (e.g. pelleted chicken manure, comfrey or seaweed based liquid feeds), but it is better and less time consuming in the end to keep the soil in good health by applying large volumes of organic material at strategic points in the cycle, so that most crops grow well most of the time

without the gardener making any specific effort to feed them.
There are 4 basic ways of achieving this:

- Bringing in farmyard or stable manure

- Making garden compost on site

- Buying commercial composts from the garden centre or mail order

- Growing and incorporating green manure crops.

The reality is that since each method has both its pros and cons, a combination of methods is usually adopted by most growers to suit their individual needs and preferences. The merits of each are discussed in the following paragraphs.

Using Animal Manure

Animal manure, whether from the farmyard or stable, is an excellent source of plant nutrients and soil enhancement. It must, however, be allowed to rot down for a period before it's used on the land. Fresh manure tends to have a burning effect on all but the most robust forms of plant life it encounters.

The challenge for us is to find a source of manure, transport it and get it spread on the land. All of these can be a time consuming and heavy task, added to which most of us would prefer not to fill up our cars with animal excrement! If you are using an allotment the easiest solution is probably to ask fellow plot holders, who may well know of a local farmer or equestrian enterprise willing to deliver by the trailer load directly to the allotment site. It may even be possible to share a large load with other allotmenteers. The question of how much is required is one of those 'piece of string questions'. An old gardening book of mine recommends 10lbs per square yard. If my maths is correct this would require 81.375 kg on each of my 15m^2 beds, but I would never dream of recommending anything so prescriptive. Obviously, the state of the soil and the quality and water content of the manure can vary considerably. However, it does give an indication of the sort of quantities to look for.

Ideally I would look to manure one of my 3 beds really well each winter, the one which will have the potatoes during the next season, as these are the most demanding of the 3 crops. If obtaining this relatively small amount of manure (for a farmer to deliver!) every year becomes difficult, an alternative would be to buy a larger quantity one year in three and to spread two thirds of it on the two empty beds. The final third can be stored under plastic or in plastic sacks on the spare ground until the remaining bed becomes free next autumn. The manure should be stored out of the rain to prevent the nutrients being washed out.

Garden Compost

A great deal has been written on how to produce good garden compost, most of which I don't propose to repeat here. However, given patience and a good supply of weeds, grass cuttings and crop debris from the plot, with the possible addition of kitchen waste, cardboard and junk mail etc. from home, a modest supply can be produced very easily, even on a small plot. The great things about it are that it's highly nutritious for the crops, it's free and it's produced on the plot so it doesn't have to be transported (if you ignore the small weekly additions of household waste). To my mind one has to do something with the weeds and surplus parts of crop plants grown on the plot, so why not compost them and return the nutrients to the soil?

The challenge with compost is to produce enough of the stuff to meet our needs. Ideally I would like to use it as an alternative to manure and would like to use it in roughly the same quantities (about 100kg per year). Although finding 100kg of material to put into the compost bin is achievable, it will soon become apparent that a large proportion, presumably moisture, is lost in the decomposition process. From what I can see it is not possible to produce enough garden compost from the waste material from any plot of land to meet the entire fertility needs of that same plot. A valuable contribution can be made and a method of disposing of the waste material ethically is needed, but garden compost made on the plot will only ever be a partial solution to the problem.

As a compromise, when I haven't organised the fertility addition as perhaps I should have done, but need to get a crop (e.g. the potatoes) in straight away, I simply put what garden compost I've got in the planting holes or trenches for the crop. This will give the crop in question some extra nutrients but will not really maintain the nutrient levels in the soil on a long term sustainable basis. If this is the only addition to fertility made over the growing cycle, then ultimately the soil will end up being depleted and all crops will suffer, but clearly it's still better than nothing.

As very busy people we all need quick fixes from time to time, but we have to remember to go back and add further compost, manure or whatever, preferably before the next crop.

Commercial Manures & Soil Improvers

A range of such products is available from garden centres and by mail order. They tend to be more concentrated than either home-made products or strawy farmyard manures. As a result they don't add the bulk that other products do, but at least this reduces the effort needed to transport them to your site. The obvious disadvantage is the fact that they have to be bought by the bagful. As a result it is an area which I have to confess to having under-researched, being possibly too mean to invest heavily in products that can be replaced by cheaper and even free alternatives. Also, as an organic grower, I would only be prepared to consider organic products. This reduces the range and increases the price of the product. I also don't particularly like the carbon implications of using a heavy, bulky product that has been transported half way around the country before it reaches me.

If I were to use a commercial product I'd look for something to add a decent bulk which also gives a slow release of nutrients over a long period. This would be used to replace the farmyard manure ahead of the potatoes in the Basic Plan.

Having complained about the cost of this approach, if it's only to be used on one 15m² bed each year, it's unlikely to break the bank and may well offer a convenient and time saving approach. At the time of writing several organic soil improvers are available at around £10-15 for a 40 litre bag, which according to their manufacturers should be adequate for one 15m² bed. What is less clear is whether this is thought to be sufficient for the 3 year cycle or merely for the year in question. This is not an area which I've really tested out, but would suggest if a commercial soil improver is used on the bed prior to planting potatoes each year, it should be supplemented with a generous application of garden compost prior to the planting of the beans, sweetcorn and squashes. This should provide an effective and time efficient solution, readily available to most growers.

Green Manure Crops

Green manures are crops grown not for harvest but for their benefits to the soil. These benefits can take the form of nutrient replacement, increase of humus content and improvement of soil structure. The plants grow quickly and help to crowd out potential weeds and in doing so they help to protect the soil, reduce compaction and leaching of nutrients due to heavy rain. When they are eventually dug in they decompose to increase the organic humus content of the soil. Many also have the ability to use deep root systems to mine the sub-soil for nutrients and trace elements that will be made available to the next crop once the green manure has been dug in. Some crops grown for this purpose also belong to the legume group and so have the ability to fix nitrogen from the air, which will in turn also benefit future crops. Alternatively, green manures can be cut and composted to increase this valuable resource but this, of course, is another task and a further complication to fit in.

The use of green manures is a low cost option compared to bringing in commercial organic fertiliser or even farmyard manure. It also requires no transportation and is therefore both organic and truly green from a carbon usage perspective. In a sense it represents a truly self-sufficient technique as the fertility is produced on site rather than being brought in from elsewhere.

The obvious down-side of using green manure is that it occupies precious land when our natural inclination is to grow crops to feed ourselves rather than crops to feed the land. So if this approach is going to be used it has to fill in one of the gaps in our plan. In doing so it has to occupy the ground over winter as this is principally when it is free. It is obviously unrealistic to expect any seed to germinate and any young plant to thrive in the depths of winter, whether it be a food crop or a green manure. The secret therefore is to get the green manure underway while there is still some warmth left in the soil in the autumn, and also to pick hardy crops that will survive harsh weather and will actively grow during any milder spells. Field beans, for example, are a good, hardy green manure option that can be sown quite late in the autumn, after summer crops have been removed. Another option is to sow a green manure between the rows of maturing summer crops so that it is well established by the time the main crop is harvested and well able to survive the winter. An example of this practice would be to sow trefoil between sweetcorn plants in late August, leaving it to grow until the following spring. In this example the sweetcorn could be cut down in the autumn for tidiness, but not up-rooted until the green manure is dug in the following March or April. Both trefoil and field beans are legumes and so they will also provide a good nitrogen boost to the soil.

One problem with establishing a green manure crop from seed in later summer can be lack of water. Clearly, as time starved gardeners who struggle to find time to water our precious food crops, we aren't going to have time to spare to water the green manure. The only approach has to be to wait for a period of rain before sowing and to pick a green manure that can cope with being sown in September. With the milder autumns we've frequently experienced in recent years there should still be time for it to establish and thrive before the cold weather hits.

There is a wide range of potential green manure crops to choose from, offering seeds to suit a range of growing seasons and conditions. Some grow tall and produce a great mass of material to dig into the soil, while others are more low-growing and more suited to under sowing another crop. Obviously no one plant species can offer all the desired benefits. Some green manures are intended for land that will be out of cultivation for a complete growing season, which is a luxury I've so far not felt able to consider. These might be worth considering if you have more land than you can handle, you need to temporarily suspend your gardening activities or if the plot you inherit is particularly poor and run down.

One other factor to consider is that a few green manures (e.g. rye grasses) are really intended for the farmer who has the equipment to plough them in at the end of the cycle. The thick, grassy sward produced presents a real challenge to the time-strapped gardener, armed only with a spade, which he could well do without. The key questions I would ask on selecting a green manure are as follows:

- What exactly am I attempting to achieve in growing this crop (e.g. is it just a quick boost to fertility before the next crop of potatoes, or do I want it to protect the soil from winter leaching)?

- How long do I have available and what time of year will it be?

- Can I get a bit of extra time by sowing the green manure around the previous crop (under sowing)?

- How will it fit in the crop rotation with previous and future crops? (see Enhancing the Plan in Chapter 4 and the list of crops by family)

Having asked these questions a good, if not always an ideal green manure, can usually can be found. A little experimentation may also be necessary in order to come up with the best candidate for any given situation.

For our purpose of trying to maintain the fertility of our plot and make the Basic Plan sustainable we need to be realistic. Green manure is yet another crop which needs to be worked into the plan; it needs the ground preparing, it needs sowing, possibly watering and ultimately harvesting or digging in. To the organic grower, ideologically, it's a great idea, but to the new gardener struggling to find time for the basics, it may be a step too far. If it is to be attempted I would suggest a simple pack of proprietary 'mixed green manure seed – for spring sowing' raked in in March and dug in before the beans, squashes and corn are planted out in late May. Alternatively, similar mixtures are available for use in the autumn. In our Basic Plan, assuming no further enhancements have been undertaken, such a green manure would fit in after the onions have been lifted.

This chapter set out to outline the products and procedures by which our Basic Plan can be developed from a one-off activity to a continuous and sustainable cycle. A range of techniques have been suggested which offer numerous options to achieve this aim. The next section outlines a number of approaches to improving the Plan to add both interest and variety, while maintaining the sustainability discussed here.

Chapter Four
Enhancing the Plan

Let's start with a pictorial representation of our Basic Plan as it applies to any one of the three Beds over a 3 year period.

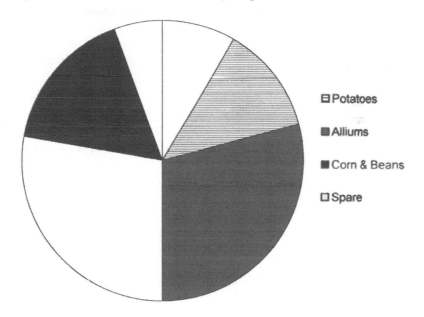

On seeing things presented like this the first reaction is usually to the empty space it graphically demonstrates; surely I can make better use of the land than this! In particular the huge gap between July in year 2 to May in year 3 really must be useable, without too much extra effort. This logic is undeniable since in July there is plenty of growing season available, there is space in the ground and time to work it. All that currently needs attention is the potato harvest on one other plot, while the beans and corn should be growing away on the third plot with very little attention.

Establishing a new crop in July isn't as easy at it might first appear, since on average July in the UK is the hottest and driest month of the year. Plants that are already established survive or, in some cases, thrive under these conditions, but new seedlings may require more support than we have available. In these circumstances delaying a new crop is an option, but we are already down to less than 3 months of growing season left, so a long delay may not give time for the new crop to reach maturity.

Given these factors, and having taken the decision to delay planting until the weather breaks, there are two growing strategies worth considering: grow a quick maturing crop which should mature before first frosts (preferably something not too frost sensitive, so that, if the timing is a little out, the whole thing isn't ruined), or grow a crop which will stand over winter and be ready for harvest next spring. This second case is only possible because in our plan the gap extends through to mid-May, when the next crop of corn and beans need to go in.

If trying the quick crop approach, quite a variety of suitable candidates are available, such as lettuce, turnips, spinach, beetroot, kohl rabi, Florence fennel, and Chinese cabbages, all with a view to getting another harvest before the end of the current growing season. Most seed packets and many catalogues provide a good indication of how long a crop will take from sowing to harvest, so it's simply a question of estimating how much growing season is left. The first frost signals the end of the growing season for most crops, but many will stand a light frost without serious damage. For the purposes of working out whether there is time left to raise a crop I usually work on growing up to the end of September, regarding anything after this as a bonus. Further North and East this may be a little optimistic.

However, the success of starting off a new crop in high summer will depend on the availability of water, so if the ground is very dry it may be worth waiting for a good downpour before sowing. In hot July weather it is unlikely that seedlings will survive on just a weekly watering. The simple solution is to keep the transplants at home, potting on as necessary, watering daily as required and to only plant them out when the weather changes. Strongly growing and reasonably large pot grown transplants will cope with longer gaps between waterings than will tiny seedlings and so, unless you are very unlucky with the weather, the approach should work well.

The other major approach is to start off a new crop which will stand over the coming winter and provide a harvest in early spring, after which it can be removed before the beans and sweetcorn are planted out in May. Spring or winter brassicas are the easiest group of crops to grow in this way. There is still time to grow spring cabbages from seed after the onion crop has been lifted or, alternatively, pot grown transplants of winter kale or purple flowering broccoli can be planted out. I've found these two produce reasonable crops with very little effort. Winter cabbages and Brussels sprouts are also possible grown as transplants, but I've found them more prone to pest damage and generally needing more care.

Whether using transplants for autumn or spring harvest, it's worth remembering that a wide range of seedlings are available by mail order these days. The quality of these seedlings is generally very high, but they are not a cheap way of producing vegetables. This approach clearly saves our precious time when compared with raising our own plants from seed, but it is normally necessary to order them some weeks in advance so, as usual, planning is required. It may also be worth ordering the seedlings to arrive a few weeks ahead of planting time and potting them on to create larger, sturdier plants.

Spring cabbages are normally sown in a seedbed in July or August and then planted out into the plot in September or October. I prefer to raise them in pots or modules outdoors, but at home where I can keep them watered and pest free without too much effort and only take them to the plot at planting out time. Planting in September makes much more sense than in July as a completely dry September is extremely rare.

A slightly more complex method of making better use of the land within our Basic Plan over this period involves being a bit cleverer about how the onion crop is planted. It is therefore best planned almost a year in advance! By leaving the occasional gap in the rows of onion sets space is left when these are planted in September. Brassica seedlings (usually Brussels sprouts, purple flowering broccoli, or winter kale) can then be inserted when they are growing strongly next May. These are left in place when the onions are lifted in June or July and will produce their own harvest between December and April, depending on the variety chosen. Obviously the number of onions produced will be slightly reduced, but overall the total harvest will be greater. I normally plant onion sets roughly 20cm apart in the row with 40 cm between rows. If opting for this approach I would miss out a set on alternate rows to create gaps of around 40 x 80 cm, but would probably only create about a dozen such spaces in the entire bed. This would clearly lose a few onions, but given the size of the plot I'll still manage to fit in the 2 bags of 50 sets I normally buy and probably still squeeze in a few garlic bulbs as well. In selecting crops to interplant in the onion bed I would choose strongly growing varieties of brassicas. If growing broccoli this way be sure to pick an early variety so that the ground will be clear in time for the next crop. Whatever brassica is chosen I would produce pot grown seedlings for transplanting rather than growing them in a seed bed on the plot.

A variation on this theme would be to create holes in the onion bed by harvesting a few of them for early use and then planting them up as described. It might be particularly handy if some of the onions start to bolt in May, as they won't grow much more if this happens.

The Next Stage

Having taken advantage of the large gap in the Basic Plan to grow a further crop, our fourth in the three year cycle, it's time to move on and examine the plan as it now stands in greater depth. We are now producing four standard crops (or five if we count beans and corn separately) in a highly time efficient manner, but although we've made a significant impact on some aspect of our diet, the crops are rather limited and perhaps unexciting. A greater variety would certainly be ideal.

There is, however, one further factor we need to produce a repeatable system of growing which can be re-used year after year. As observed at the end of the discussion on the Basic Plan, it is generally accepted that a 3 year rotation is too short and risks diminution of key minerals in the soil and the build up of crop specific pests and diseases. This is not a hypothesis that I've ever tested. It could well be that given good application of manure and or compost at appropriate points in the cycle (certainly pre-potato planting at least), the Basic Plan might yield well for many years. On balance though, I think it best to go with conventional wisdom and enhance the plan from year 4 onwards, so that the gap between successive crops of the same type or family on the same ground is extended. The minimum acceptable rotation is usually taken as four years, but many gardeners prefer longer.

Firstly, it should be taken as read that enhancement/replacement of soil fertility will need to be in place by this stage. The holiday period, if there was one, will now be over and nutrients being removed in the harvest must be replaced if productivity is to be maintained. All the options were set out in the previous chapter, but whichever one is chosen, it needs to be fitted in with any more complex growing patten.

So what changes should we make to the crops in order to make the plan both sustainable and, hopefully, more interesting? As usual the key decision here is how much time is available. It should be remembered that the Basic Plan was constructed around a set of crops which required minimum effort to grow, which were from different botanical families to allow a safe rotation and which could be harvested either as required or in bulk to suit the needs of the busy gardener. Whatever crops are added to the plan the amount of work involved will increase, and in many cases significantly, but there are a number of options available.

The first and easiest option is to simply remove one of the three crops from the rotation and replace it with another crop, or group of crops. By removing a different one of the original crops each year a 4 year rotation is achieved across the 3 bed system, as shown below. The choice available is still reasonable, but the point is to avoid the families of vegetables already featuring in our rotation. So far we have potatoes (solenacea), onions (allium), kale/broccoli (brassica), and beans (legume)/sweetcorn (gramineae). A bed can contain a mixture of crops or families, as we have done with the beans, sweetcorn and pumpkins group, but we don't really want to repeat any members of the existing groups.

My choice for the fourth group of crops in the rotation I've called simply 'roots', and in this category I include a mixture of carrots, parsnips, beetroot and Swiss Chard or leaf beet. Once again they are a group of crops from several different families, but they fit together well, can be sown at much the same time and cope with similar conditions. The other thing they have in common is not being members of the botanical families already represented elsewhere in the rotation. All of them, except the parsnips, can be harvested as required over the later summer and early autumn. The parsnips will stand over winter and only need to be cleared in time for digging the ground for the next crop. Although this is a slightly messy group of crops it really shouldn't be too much extra work. It would probably be simpler to fill the plot with just one or two crops, but this would result in more parsnips, for example, than I could possibly use and we have already agreed that this would be self-defeating.

Although I've called this group root crops, the important facts are that they fit together well with regard to space and work requirements and that they represent new botanical families in the rotation. I've not included Swedes and turnips as they are brassicas, but these could be also be included in the root crops group if the option of including other brassicas in the rotation was not taken up. The fact that not all of the new group are actually roots is immaterial. Under this scheme the plan for the next 4 years might look like this:

	Year 4	Year 5	Year 6	Year 7
Bed 1	Roots	Alliums followed by brassicas	Sweet-corn, drying beans, pumpkins	Potatoes
Bed 2	Sweetcorn, drying beans, pumpkins	Potatoes	Roots	Alliums followed by brassicas
Bed 3	Alliums followed by brassicas	Roots	Potatoes	Sweetcorn, drying beans, pumpkins

Notice that I've also included the option of growing winter brassicas in the long gap between harvesting the onions in July and planting the next crop the following spring. If the sweetcorn, beans and pumpkins group is still the follow-on, as it was in the Basic Plan, there is plenty of time for the brassicas. If the roots follow the brassicas, a little more fiddling may become necessary, but it's still quite possible. When this happens I would clear the brassicas, dig the ground and sow the roots in stages. This way I can plant the parsnip seeds in March while there is still some purple flowering broccoli in the plot, and then sow the carrots and other roots after the last of the brassicas have been cleared – probably late April.

Overall, the downside of a plan like this is that we only produce 3 out of our 4 groups of crops each year (or 4 out of 5 counting the winter brassicas separately), but at least we now have a sustainable system. This may appear rather a blow, but when we consider what we are now producing, if all the options have been included, the list is quite impressive. Taking Year 4 as an example, Bed 1 will produce carrots, parsnips, beetroot and leaf beet, Bed 2 will provide sweetcorn, drying beans and pumpkins and Bed 3 will give us onions and garlic, followed by kale and sprouting broccoli. Overall this must be regarded as a reasonable selection from a fairly modest area of land and at a reasonably low level of effort.

This may well provide an acceptable solution to many, but there's no getting round the fact that in one year in four there will be no potatoes, in another year there will be no onions, and so on. If this is not acceptable, the simplest solution is to keep to broadly the same set of crops, but to divide each bed in half and give a six year rotation along the lines of the diagram over the page

	Year 1	Year 2	Year 3	Year 4	Year 5	Year 6
Jan		plus garlic and/or leeks				
Feb						
Mar	Second Early Pota-toes					
April						
May			Drying beans	Roots (pars-nips, carrots etc)	Sweet-corn	Pump-kins
June						
July						
Aug		Brassi-cas (bro-colli & kale)				
Sept	Over win-tering onions					
Oct						
Nov						
Dec						

This plan, I would suggest, offers the combination of sustainability, an acceptable rotation without crops coming round too fast, a reasonable variety of produce and not too heavy a work load. It offers a fair degree of further flexibility, principally within the roots and brassicas plot, to change and perhaps increase the variety each year, while retaining the minimum effort basic crops elsewhere. Additionally, since alliums still follow potatoes, a few seedling leeks could be planted as the first of the potatoes are lifted to add further variety to this group.

Clearly the permutations here are almost infinite and any final decisions will come down to personal preferences. Some thoughts on each individual crop and how they may be used and fitted in to the bigger plan are contained in the Crop Selection Chapter, but a few general guidelines are as follows:

▪ Don't make it too complicated to start with – a few crops grown well are a much better use of your valuable time than a lot more grown badly.

▪ Think through the details, including cultivation and harvest, before planting – it saves time and reduces failures.

- Remember seedlings can be bought from garden centres and by mail order – this saves both your time and time occupying the ground.

- When planting out, try to plant out good sized, vigorously growing seedlings – they will give you less work.

- If unsure, start with some of the minimal effort crops described in the plans above and then add/substitute a few of your own preferences as time goes by.

- Remember to use the plant group lists contained in the appendices to ensure a good rotation is followed.

When the ideas set out in this chapter to enhance the Basic Plan are implemented, the plot described at the start will have changed considerably; some of the big blocks of empty space will have gone, the monoculture beds will have been reduced in size and new crops added to create variety.

The No-Dig Variation (or At Least Low Dig!)

Having taken the option to step up to a six bed system with a relatively long crop rotation, it's well worth considering exactly how this is implemented. It may be tempting to simply cut each of the 5 metre x 3 metre beds in half to create six beds of 2.5 metres x 3m metres (or a little less, allowing for paths). These almost square beds are not the most convenient to work, as it is still hard to reach the middle of each without walking on the soil. My suggestion in this situation is to create six long narrow beds (say 5 metres x 1.2 metres) and work on the principle of tending them entirely from the paths. This will reduce soil compaction markedly, consequently reducing the amount of digging required. Such a plan may work best if the beds are edged with timber which will clearly add time and expense, but which once set up, should need a minimum of attention for many years. The idea is that digging is kept to a minimum and that the soil surface is constantly fed with organic material to keep it in good health. The additions are kept to the beds only, not the paths, and so none is wasted. When the beds are not in use they should be kept covered by a mulch, organic or otherwise, or a green manure crop can be grown.

A great deal has been said and written about no-dig vegetable growing in recent years. I don't propose to repeat most of it here, but there are a couple of salient points worth making. Firstly, I'm only introducing the idea in the latter stages of the plans, as I believe that no-dig only has a reasonable chance of success once the ground is clear of perennial weeds – don't try it too soon. Secondly, some light digging will usually be necessary from time to time, particularly when growing on a heavy, clay based soil. It is possible to grow potatoes under a mulch, but most of us are happier to bury them in the soil in the usual way. I would personally, therefore, prefer to think in terms of low-dig rather than no-dig, but it is undoubtedly a very useful technique in the armoury of the time starved gardener.

If More Land Becomes Available….

If more growing space becomes available or you simply find a way of squeezing in a seventh bed, an alternative angle is well worth considering.

We all know that the difficult and time consuming thing about growing pretty much any crop is usually getting the plants established. With most crops we spend most of our time cultivating, protecting and generally enabling the tiny seedling to turn itself into a mature plant. Once it has done so it is generally a fairly easy step from there to harvesting the finished crop, whether that crop is fruit, leaves, shoots, or even roots. It therefore makes sense for us to pay attention to those crops which, once established, yield their produce year after year. These perennial vegetables usually need little attention once growing but are, as a group, generally much less effort than their annual equivalents. They may take a year or two to produce anything worthwhile, but when this is set against anything up to 20 years of easy production, it is simply amazing that they aren't more widely grown.

The list of true perennial vegetables available to most growers is not large: typically limited to asparagus, globe artichokes, sea kale and possibly Good King Henry, the poor man's asparagus. However there are also a number of useful crops which can be grown as if they were perennials (i.e. plant once but harvest many times). The most obvious of these is the Jerusalem artichoke. The tubers of this plant can be planted in the later winter, allowed to grow and reproduce throughout the next growing season and then most of the crop can be harvested during the following winter. This leaves a small proportion of the crop in the ground to produce the next generation of plants and tubers during the following season. I've known people claim to have maintained an artichoke bed in this way for 20 years.

There are other crops which, although normally grown as annuals, can survive into subsequent seasons and produce a useful crop with no effort from the gardener at all. Chard, leaf beets and some chicories fall into this category.

The downside of most perennial crops is that they occupy quite a large area of land year in, year out in return for providing a fairly modest amount of edible/marketable crop. This may not be a bad thing if you've got a large allotment or garden and not enough time to cultivate it in the conventional way. However, from the point of view of the commercial producer this does not prove an acceptable investment. I suspect that it is for this superficial reason that perennial crops do not play a major part in most of our diets. Very little time and money has been invested in developing the range of perennial crops currently available and breeding new strains. For example, 9 Star Perennial Broccoli and Dorbenton's Perennial Kale are very useful crops for the time constrained gardener, but neither are perfect or last long enough to be truly classed as perennial. There must be immense scope for breading strains of perennial, or at least multi-seasonal brassicas, but I don't see the seed companies lining up to be the first in this field.

Chapter Five
Crop Selection

There are no absolute golden rules about what the time starved grower should select for inclusion in his/her garden. However, there is a huge variation in the amount of time and care different crops require to produce a worthwhile harvest. Most varieties will benefit from extra care and attention, but this is not our concern here; we need to be very careful about planting anything that requires a lot of our time to be productive.

Having looked at growing systems as a whole, this section discusses the pros and cons of growing individual vegetable crops in terms of the effort required to obtain a reasonable yield. It also gives some pointers as to the easiest ways of using each and suggests some basic techniques to optimise production, while minimising effort. This is clearly going to be one of the two main factors in the time pressed gardener's choice of crops. The other is personal preference: there is clearly no point in growing something if we don't want to eat it ourselves. One of the effects of combining these two factors is that, although I've grown all the vegetables discussed at some time or other, where I've found something difficult and have not been particularly keen on it, I've not usually persevered with it. The lesson here is simple; if you are particularly keen on a crop, experiment with it. If you eat a lot of celery, for example, grow it on a small scale. Experiment with timings, growing conditions, location, and protection etc., until you find a way of producing it in a way that meets your needs without dominating your time.

Having assessed the benefits of each individual crop it is then a matter of deciding how combinations of crops can be put together into the kind of system we have explored to complete an achievable, useful and sustainable cropping plan.

Artichoke, Globe

These are easy plants to produce, but occupy the ground for a long time (they are short-lived perennials) and don't give a huge yield considering the space they take up. Seedlings raised or bought in spring need to be planted out at wide spacings (about a metre each way) and should produce a modest crop of edible flower buds late in their first summer, or early in their second spring depending on the weather. In fact they can produce a useful spring crop when there isn't much else around. Some protection may be required to get them through a harsh winter, but if this is done successfully a larger crop should follow the following year. The only real effort involved in producing this crop occurs in producing and planting out the seedlings and keeping down competing weeds in their first year. The size of the plants means that weeds are much less of a problem in later years. It is a warm climate crop which dislikes water logging but is able to survive dry periods, so watering should not be a chore. Once established in the garden the best way of maintaining production is to select side shoots from existing vigorous plants, remove them and plant them on as new plants. If left in situ they will take over from the parent plants as these die back.

Artichoke, Jerusalem

This is a lazy gardener's dream; a true 'plant and forget it' crop. They can be planted in late winter one year, ignored all summer, cut down in autumn and the tubers harvested and the ground cleared during the following winter. To take it one stage further, a permanent bed can be established where most of the tubers are lifted each winter, with a few left to establish the next year's crop. If this is done occasional boosts to fertility will be required, such as a good covering of manure laid over the whole bed in winter every few years. The only point to remember is that the majority of the tubers must be lifted each year. If you forget about them completely the plants will become over crowded and the size of the tubers will diminish markedly. One other labour saving tip is to select a smooth skinned variety like Fuseau. This will save time in the kitchen as peeling artichokes can be harder work than growing them.

Artichoke, Chinese

Chinese artichokes are very similar to Jerusalem artichokes, with smaller, pearly white tubers which are grown in the same way. These tubers have the advantage of being much thinner skinned and so a scrubbing rather than a peeling will usually suffice before cooking, thus alleviating the most tedious aspect of this crop. Most growers feel that the Chinese version has a superior flavour to the Jerusalem artichoke.

Asparagus

Asparagus is a true perennial, so once established and provided with a modest amount of care, it should carry on cropping for 15-20 years. Taking the long-term view then, it is an ideal crop for the time-starved grower. The easiest way of establishing it is to buy one-year-old plants, or crowns, which are easily available each spring from mail order suppliers. They can be grown from seed, but this is an unnecessary task and will simply delay the production of the first crop by a further year. Plants established from bought in crowns or seedlings will produce a small crop one year after planting and will be in full production by the following year. This may appear a long time to wait, but the work to be done in the mean time is not great. It is really just a question of keeping the weeds down. Watering if a dry spell occurs during the first summer is probably a good idea, but once the plants are well established they appear able to come through a drought without our help. The only remaining task is cutting the crop each May and June. This is scarcely a chore, although rapid growth rates in warm weather may make it necessary to visit the plot at least twice a week if all the emerging spears are to be caught at an optimum size. However, the season is short, no more than 8 weeks in fact, and it's not disastrous if a few spears are missed. If this happens it's best to cut the overgrown spears and discard them to encourage the plants to produce more.

Aubergine

This is best regarded as strictly a greenhouse or polytunnel crop. Whilst it is possible to raise a few plants without protection they require a sheltered spot, a good summer and a lot of cosseting. If you really like aubergines and have a sunny patio it is perfectly possible grow a few in pots. From my experience the results are unlikely to be proportionate to the time and effort required, but if it's only a case of investing the odd 5 minutes most days it can be fun to try them on this scale.

Beans, Broad

These are an easy low effort crop to produce. The large and fairly robust seeds make this one of the few crops I sow directly into the ground, rather than transplanting. An early spring sowing will produce a crop in June or July depending on the variety chosen. However, because there is always a lot do on the vegetable plot in spring, I usually choose a really hardy variety (like Aquadulce Claudia) and sow in November. This gives me a crop in early June or even late May, which is great as I tend to be short on produce at that time of year. If you are really pressed for time it's worthwhile thinking like this to try and ensure that the work is spread as evenly as possible throughout the year.

The only disadvantage with broad beans is that if they are left too long on the plants the beans tend to become hard and develop tough skins. These can be removed before cooking, but it's a job the cook could do without. The objective is therefore to pick the pods as soon as they mature, which requires frequent checking. Immature pods can also be picked and cooked whole, but obviously many more will be required to make a decent meal. It is only the harvesting that presents the grower with any real burden as it is not a plant that is particularly fussy about either its planting or subsequent care. Also, as its main growing period is the spring, the ground usually contains enough water. I don't think I've ever bothered watering this crop.

Beans, French

French beans come in two basic types; climbing and dwarf. Dwarf French beans tend to crop slightly earlier than the climbing ones, but the climbers will usually produce a heavier crop from each plant. The only real difference in the effort required to produce them is the obvious point that if we wish to go for the climbing variety, we have to go to the trouble of creating some kind of structure for them to climb up. This is not particularly difficult, but does usually necessitate obtaining a pole of wood or bamboo 2 metres ore more in length for each plant. Most commentators insist that beans climb much better up poles than they do up strings, although personally I've not found much difference. One further point to note with tall climbers like these beans is that they will shade the ground to at least one side of them. It's therefore important to think about where they are sited on the plot and the direction of the rows to ensure that their impact on other crops is minimised.

French beans of either kind are tender plants and will not grow away under cold conditions. Many gardeners put in a lot of time and effort to try and get them underway as early as possible. With our style of gardening this is not realistic, nor, to be honest, can I see much point in it. Wait until the conditions are really favourable before planting out home grown or bought in seedlings. It's much easier to protect the seedlings in pots or root trainers than it is to protect them in the open garden once they've been planted out. Also, it's better to delay the harvest very slightly by planning to plant out late than it is to lose the plants and have to waste time getting more. Even here in my garden in relatively mild Somerset I didn't get my climbing beans in last year until 22nd May, but they grew away quickly in the warm weather and still produced a good crop.

Once French beans are growing well they shouldn't give many problems. They like warm weather and will survive a drought well. However, they will produce a better crop if watered. It is only the picking that can cause problems if you are short of time. These beans will usually continue to crop as long as the beans are picked, or until it becomes too cold in the autumn. If you fail to pick the beans for a couple of weeks in the middle of the season, there is a danger that the existing pods will become large, tough and mature, and that the plant will feel that it's done its job and its seed is set. It will then cease to flower even if these mature pods are removed and your bean season will be over. To keep the plants producing it's best to pick them at least twice each week, which can be a challenge to the time-starved grower.

Beans, Drying

Drying beans are simply varieties of French beans selected for their ability to produce mature beans rather than immature bean pods. There are a number of dual-purpose varieties which can be picked as either fresh green beans, or later as dried beans. However, I prefer to keep the two crops separate, as removal of some of the potential drying beans as green beans may delay their replacements and so some of the drying crop may mature too late to dry and store effectively. But most importantly, this really is a 'plant and forget it' crop. Once it's in and growing away there is nothing to do until it's ready for harvest. They can, if it suits you, all be planted on a single day in May and can then all be harvested in one day towards the end of September. Watering in dry spells will increase the yield, but left completely alone a reasonable crop will result.

Drying beans are available in both climbing and dwarf forms. I prefer to grow climbing varieties for drying, as they get the pods up in the air where they can dry much better and are out of the way of autumnal slugs. Also, as with French beans, the yield per plant is slightly higher.

When it comes to harvesting the beans it is important to pick them in as dry a state as possible. The beans should be left to dry on the plants, as far as possible, and then brought in and the drying completed in a warm place. It goes without saying that a couple of days of dry weather is really needed prior to picking. What is not so obvious, though, is that mature but still green beans do not dry easily from scratch in a warm room or an airing cupboard at home. Sometimes a grey mould can develop on them. If you are having difficulties in getting the beans dried it is better to pull up the entire plants and hang them to dry slowly in a cool shed or garage for about a month before removing the beans, and only then to remove and shell the beans, and finally to dry them indoors in the usual way.

It may also be worth harvesting some of the crop for use as fresh flageolet beans. These are simply the mature beans harvested while the pods are still fresh and green. If a proportion of the crop is used in this way in the late summer or early autumn, there is less effort needed in drying and storing the remainder. It is also possible to freeze fresh flageolet beans if drying is inconvenient.

Runner Beans

Runner beans are similar in many respects to climbing French beans. They will produce a heavy crop for eating as green pods containing the immature beans in late summer and early autumn. So long as planting is left until conditions are warm enough, the only challenges are watering and picking. Overly dry conditions will result in a much reduced crop and a tendency for the beans to rapidly become tough and stringy. Also, frequent picking is required to maintain constant production of new young pods. As a consequence of these two factors and the fact that my own family aren't that keen on these beans, I don't tend to grow that many of them.

If you are going to grow them I would recommend using a modern variety that claims to produce stringless pods (e.g. Butler). The reality is that every variety I've tried will produce stringy pods if left on the plants too long or not watered enough, but these stringless varieties can put up with more bad treatment than the older varieties and they will therefore be more appropriate to our plans. I would suggest it's worth growing a relatively small quantity of runner beans to add variety at the end of the season, but personally I find it hard to understand the desire to create the huge double rows so often found on our allotment sites.

Beetroot

An easy crop and one which I would certainly recommend growing in at least modest quantities. Beetroot is one of those crops where conventional wisdom recommends frequent sowing in small quantities. I regard this as too much trouble and so look for a method and a variety whereby a single sowing can supply my needs over a protracted period. For this to work the sowing needs to be left slightly later (around May) and a variety resistant to bolting should be selected. In theory, I aim to space the plants so that some baby beets can be harvested as thinnings and the rest of the crop left to mature to full size. In reality things don't always work out so neatly, but it's a good principle to aim for.

An alternative, easy approach is simply to grow for a single autumn harvest and to store the crop after that. The timing and variety for this may need a little experimentation, but it is an excellent plan if you like pickled beetroot or you have space to store the beets whole, as they keep quite well given the appropriate cool conditions. Clearly, if you are going for a mass pickling exercise the harvest can be planned for any time that suits a busy lifestyle, but if storage of the whole roots is planned, the harvest must be late enough to ensure cool weather.

Broccoli, Purple or White Sprouting

This is a particularly useful vegetable to grow and one that can be made productive on a modest scale with very little effort. The great thing about it from the gourmet's perspective is that it is a source of fresh tasty greens in early spring, when there's not much else available. From the grower's point of view too it's useful as it does much of its growing in the autumn and spring when there's much less competition for space, but the plants do occupy the ground for a long time.

It isn't difficult to raise the plants from seed, but I usually can't be bothered to look after them from a spring sowing to the size when they are ready to plant out. I therefore usually buy seedlings in modules and plant them out in mid to late summer, after the ground has been cleared from an earlier crop (e.g. onions or garlic planted the previous autumn). These seedlings usually grow away easily, just needing a bit of watering to get them started and in any prolonged dry periods. They will have turned into sturdy plants by the time of the first frosts, but will continue to put on growth during any milder spells. The harvestable flower buds usually start to appear in March, as the weather begins to warm up. The plants can be left to their own devices from September, or earlier if the summer is a damp one, right through to harvesting the following spring. The cutting of the immature buds can be continued for at least 4 weeks as the plants will continue to produce new spikes as the old ones are removed. This is a fairly slow re-growth and so a weekly cut will usually be enough to keep the supply going and avoid the buds opening into flowers and hence being wasted.

The only serious problem I have encountered with this crop is that over the winter the green leaves and new shoots are very attractive to birds, pigeons and pheasants in particular. If these are likely to be a problem in your area it's worth covering the plants with fleece or netting or using bird scarring tapes (strung-up, not playing!). Since I would normally only grow half a dozen broccoli plants bird protection measures don't present too big a task.

Brussels Sprouts

I have to admit that this is one of the few crops that I'm still working on in the low effort garden. The long growing season and a susceptibility to pests tend to combine into making it a demanding crop. Slugs, cabbage white butterflies, a range of aphids and birds, particularly pigeons, all in their turn like to graze on the growing plants. It's all too easy to end up with plants too badly damaged to produce much of a crop. I've also, at times, ended up with a crop of open, rather loose bunches of small leaves rather than the tight buttons we all aim for. I understand that firmer soil with a higher organic content is likely to prevent this 'blown effect', as it's known.

The most time efficient strategy I've come up with is to buy seedling plants in modules to save dealing with tiny seedlings and to eliminate the devastating effect slugs can have on new seedlings. These seedlings can be potted on once to allow them to reach a respectable and more robust size before planting out, well watered. After this they can be enclosed within a netting or enviromesh covering and left to their own devices for most of the summer. Short, low-growing varieties will clearly be easier to protect that the taller ones. Once the weather starts cooling down in the autumn the butterfly season will be over and, unless pigeons or other birds are a particular pest, the coverings can be removed and the plants left open to harvest.

I've tried another lazy technique and this is to attempt to hide the plants on the summer plot amongst other, less attractive plants. This appears to work to a reasonable extent, with some caterpillar damage but by no means decimation and is certainly less hassle than messing around with netting, but is probably only practical when growing them on a small scale. I chose to experiment with the late cropping variety Trafalgar as I wanted a plant that would compete strongly with the cover plants.

Cabbages

Cabbages are available in a huge range of varieties, making it possible to harvest them at pretty much any time of the year. Being closely related to the Brussels sprouts discussed previously, they suffer from the same large range of pests. I find the easiest way of avoiding these is to keep the plants growing in the plot for as short a time as possible, thus minimising their exposure. Also, like the other members of the brassica family, cabbages prefer moist, heavy soils. If gardening on a clay-based soil they are usually quite easy to grow with very little effort. On a light, sandy soil, however, they can be much harder. In those circumstances it's important to improve the soil with as much organic matter as possible and to plant the seedlings deeply to ensure they are very firmly embedded.

In spring seedlings for a summer cabbage harvest can be raised or bought and planted out as soon as the ground is reasonably warm. They will then grow away quickly and need no real further care. Hardy seedlings like these could go in earlier, but the risk of succumbing to the slugs is too great. Grown this way I achieve a good crop of small summer cabbages (usually Mini Cole or Greyhound variety) with very little effort.

Seedlings of winter cabbages are best planted out in July or August, which would mean a June sowing. I'm always too busy or disorganised to do this, so I tend to buy seedlings and not get them in the ground until August, preferably waiting for a spell of wetter weather before doing so. It's easier to water seedlings in their modules in the waiting area than it is walking around the plot after they've been planted out.

Similarly, the seedlings of spring cabbages can be bought and planted out in September. Rain is usually less of a problem by September and so these can be easier to grow. As with the cabbages planted in high summer, the cabbages white butterflies are still around and protection is usually wise. Having said that, if these pests are not particularly numerous in your area, the busy gardener can just put up with hopefully modest damage and still get a reasonable return once the cabbage head is trimmed up. Spring cabbages are usually less affected in this way since the caterpillars are killed by the first frosts and the adults do not reappear until after the crop has been harvested.

Calabrese

By calabrese I mean the green summer vegetable often mis-named broccoli. It isn't particularly difficult to grow but can be rather prone to damage by butterfly caterpillars. As another member of the brassica family, it's grown in much the same way as summer cabbages. The annoying thing about it is that both we and the caterpillars both eat the flower buds of this plant and it's all too easy to miss the little grubs in the flower heads when preparing them in the kitchen. This has led to emotional scenes over Sunday lunch in the Wootton household!

In my attempts to avoid these domestic catastrophes I tried starting off the calabrese really early in the hope of getting to harvest before the butterflies were on the wing. It was then that I learned that this brassica is more frost sensitive than many of its cousins. The only solution I can find is to provide fleece or enviromesh protection. This is an extra chore, but not usually too burdensome, assuming that calabrese is only grown on a modest scale. Once the seedlings are in the ground, the protection is in place above them and the odd beer trap beneath to temp the slugs, crop can be left to its own devices until harvesting.

When selecting varieties of calabrese it's worth remembering that since we want to eat the flower buds, and the plant, presumably, wants to flower and set seed, it won't stand in an edible condition for very long. To my mind it therefore makes sense to go for an older (i.e. none-F1 hybrid) variety, as this will spread the harvest. Although a single hit harvest clearly saves time and effort, there is little value in having 30-40 odd heads of calabrese ready at once.

Carrots

In terms of soil preferences carrots are the exact opposite of cabbages, preferring light, sandy soils. I find them quite difficult to grow in my heavy clay soil. Like most root crops they need to be sown in situ, rather than being transplanted, and then thinned out to an appropriate density. The difficulty tends to be in getting them started off. My spring soil tends to remain cold for quite some time, leading to patchy germination and considerable damage from slugs. If I leave sowings until later, the soil surface has usually dried out and become hard-baked. Regular watering offers the obvious solution, but I rarely find the time. A better approach is to mix sand or fine grit into the soil in a very narrow trench and sow into this. The area improved in this way can be quite small since, once established, the carrots should be OK in less than ideal soil. Alternatively, I've had some success sowing in potting compost inside empty toilet roll tubes, thinning to a single seedling in each and planting out once each was large enough to cope. It is a bit of a fiddle but it does work, even with heavy soil and too many slugs.

My other easy solution to producing carrots is to grow them in a large pot or tub of potting compost located just outside the back door. I don't normally go for container growing as the watering involved is usually too great a commitment, but I sometimes make an exception for my tub of carrots. By locating this single tub where I can't forget it, success is more achievable. This approach clearly doesn't provide carrots as a staple of the family's winter dinner table, but it will provide a few bunches of tasty young roots in late summer.

The other great problem with carrots is the carrot root fly. The larval stage of this pest spends its time eating a network of tiny holes through the carrot roots, making them inedible. The only total solution available to the organic grower is to cover the crop with fine mesh or fleece. The busy gardener may simply opt for buying one of the resistant varieties such as Fly Away. I've found this offers a significant reduction in carrot fly damage, if not total elimination, and it does mean you don't have to do anything extra. I've also noticed that the tub by the back door is much less badly affected than the carrots grown out in the open plot. I'm also told that earthing-up young carrot plants helps to deter carrot fly. Since I've only tried it when growing Fly Away I can't really comment on whether it worked or whether the success was due to the carrot's natural resistance.

Cauliflowers

Cauliflowers are another brassica and very similar to cabbages, but rather more demanding. They need a particularly rich, heavy soil and a very good water supply. As a result they are not really the sort of crop that suits the busy grower. One particularly wet summer I saw my neighbour produce a magnificent crop with very little effort, but where these conditions can't be relied on I wouldn't invest the time and space needed for this crop.

One rather easy method worth experimenting with is to treat cauliflowers in much the same way as sprouting broccoli. If seedlings of a spring cropping variety can be bought and planted out in July or even August, the watering required to keep them going in late summer shouldn't be too great. Planting at this time would make maximum use of the wet seasons of the year to achieve good growth in autumn and again in spring.

Celery

This is another demanding crop, needing a long, frost-free growing season and continuously moist conditions. These requirements, coupled with the fact that none of my family are very keen on eating it once produced, has meant that I've never really invested the time and effort needed to grow it.

Corn Salad

Corn salad is a very useful cool or even cold season salad crop. It is very easy to grow and will withstand the coldest of conditions and, if grown at these times of year, will need very little effort (with even no need to water it most years). I would suggest growing it in pots on the patio table throughout its life. The plants are low-growing and likely to get splattered with mud if grown on the open plot. Besides, if you are growing winter salads you don't want to be walking round a muddy plot hunting for them in the dark.

Chard, Leaf Beet and Perpetual Spinach

I've treated this botanically similar collection of crops as a group since not only are they closely related, but they can be treated in much the same way both in the garden and the kitchen. They really are a very easy collection to grow and much less bother than traditional spinach, which I rarely use at all. I find that with very little effort these crops provide a continuous leaf harvest over a very long period. They will only need care and attention while at the seedling stage, principally watering in prolonged dry spells. After that the only task is harvesting. I've experimented in growing the variety Rainbow chard as if it were a perennial and found that it will produce a good crop throughout its second year. It survived its second winter but I found the vigour of the plants dramatically reduced by the third summer. Clearly more work could be done on this, but it serves to make the point that this is a superb plant for the time-starved gardener. I've had a row of chard plants producing leaf crops for most of their second season with no more effort than that taken to pick it, not to mention the cropping late into the autumn of year one.

Chicory

It is very easy to grow most varieties of green or red leafed chicories to provide a distinctive, bitter tasting element to a salad. Seeds can be sown directly into their final growing conditions or can be sown in modules and planted out. This is usually done in early summer with a view to producing leaves well into the winter, as many varieties are quite hardy. The production of this crop is not the difficult bit; it's making use of it that I find more of a challenge. It's great to add a small quantity of these bitter leaves to enhance an otherwise bland salad, but I don't want a salad of pure chicory. To co-ordinate a large number of annual salad crops to produce this balanced mix in the salad bowl is probably asking too much of the busy gardener, unless of course salads are your main interest and you aren't going to grow much else. The easy solution for the busy gardener is to buy a pack of mixed salad leaves (e.g. Saladini) which will inevitably contain some chicory as well as a selection of lettuces and probably rocket and land cress. This mixture is simply broadcast sown and the leaves cut frequently to encourage re-growth. The idea is to harvest whatever combination is available at that particular time, so the precise consistency of the salad will vary throughout the season.

One other type of chicory is sometimes known as witloof. Here the plant is grown from seed in summer, the roots are harvested in autumn, re-potted and brought into a warm, dark place. This produces a crop of new, blanched leaves, which can be eaten in a salad or as a cooked vegetable. The plants are very easy to produce from seed and will grow all summer without any attention. But it can be rather a fiddle to pot them on and to look after them indoors. If a suitable space is available, it is worth the effort, though, as it can provide a fresh crop in mid - winter when there are very few others.

Courgettes

A really easy crop to produce, but one that is even easier to turn into marrows! In warm weather a courgette plant can turn its fruit from 2cm long embryos behind the flowers to 15-20 cm long courgettes in just 2 days. If you aren't there to pick them they will carry on growing at the same rate until you do. The result is inevitably a quantity of small vegetable marrows, which is fine if that's what you like. Even if you can't use them this isn't disastrous. The offending fruit can just be thrown in the compost bin and the plants will produce more.

I usually start off courgettes from seed, as they germinate fairly easily and I get a better choice of variety than I would if I bought young plants. I always germinate the seeds on the windowsill and move the seedlings out to the patio table to harden off. It's important not to start them off too early. Cucurbits in general don't like cold weather, so it's best to leave things a bit later to be sure that they will grow away quickly when planted out. Planting out early just wastes your time, as you end up fiddling with covers and shelters, or worst of all losing the plants and having to start again. It's much better to play it safe and plant late. Here in Somerset I used the following timetable for last year's courgettes:

25 Apr	Sowed seeds in small pots on warm windowsill, variety Tempra.
1 May.	Seeds germinated
11 May.	Moved plants outside to harden off
21 May.	Planted out in plot
28 June	First fruit harvested.

The hot weather of June and July 2006 resulted in a magnificent harvest, with the only effort being keeping up with the picking. It's also worth noting that after the initial planting I only watered them once or twice during two very dry months. This really is an excellent busy gardener's crop.

Cucumbers

Although predominately a greenhouse crop, there are varieties that can be grown successfully outside. My views on greenhouses for those of us who are short of time are explained in the next chapter, so here I'll concentrate on the outdoor crops. This is clearly a crop where the busy gardener might consider growing just the odd plant. It's hard to imagine the point in growing rows of them, and personally I'm not inclined to bother. Although in some ways similar to courgettes they can be rather more troublesome, needing watering and training. Also, the fruits themselves can be disappointing, tending to develop much tougher skins as a result of unprotected growing and may become bitter if left on the plants too long.

Fennel, Florence

I've frequently found this to be a useful follow-on crop for planting out after early potatoes, peas or broad beans have been harvested. The secret, if attempting to do this, is to have seedlings ready to go in as soon as the ground is cleared of the previous crop. This would give a sowing time of early June if, for example, I was trying to follow-on after over-wintered broad beans, which could be expected to be cleared by early July. All this may be too much planning and organisation for our purposes, especially as I have rarely seen Florence Fennel for sale as seedlings to short-cut the process.

I am suggesting planting it at this point in the year because it tends to bolt if planted much earlier. Obviously, you could simply leave the space empty until July, but I always find this requires too much discipline. The only other point to make about this crop is that it really does need watering during prolonged dry spells, which can prove to be one job too many. As suggested with similarly demanding crops, if in the middle of a July drought it's probably best to delay planting out for a bit. August is often wetter than July and, unless frosts are particularly early, there should still be time for the bulbs to mature.

Recent varieties have been developed that claim to be resistant to bolting (e.g. Finale) which should make it suitable for growing at the start of the season rather than the end. I have to admit to not having tried this variety yet, but the approach should make life simpler, although the problem of water in summer dry spells remains.

Garlic

Garlic is a truly great crop for the busy gardener. It really can be grown successfully by simply planting out the individual cloves in October or November and lifting new bulbs in June or July. Use a variety selected for autumn planting (e.g. Theridrome). The only work I do to this crop between these dates is to hoe between the plants a couple of times in the spring to keep the weeds down and to scatter a few handfuls of pelleted chicken manure on them as they start to re-grow in the early spring. By being fairly generous with the spacing (I grow at 20cm in the row and 30cm between rows) I find I can produce bulbs that are much larger than those sold in the shops. A number of this year's crop exceeded 6cm in diameter and 100g in weight. I think it makes sense to grow them like this as it's much easier to hoe between the plants at this wide spacing.

Another advantage of garlic is that it can all be harvested at once, pretty much at a date to suit the grower and stored for later use. I find it keeps for almost a year, so there are no great problems with storage.

One point worth making is that it is best lifted and dried in a coolish place indoors before the top growth has completely died off. Each leaf on the upper part of the plant represents a layer of skin around the bulb. Once the top growth is dead these protective skins start dying off and eventually the bulb will disintegrate, causing the cloves to separate and allow in disease. I look to harvest my garlic when the plants appear to be about 50% brown, with the rest still green. After lifting, the loose soil is shaken off and the complete plants are bundled up, 10-12 at a time, and hung in my garage for about a month to dry. After this time they can be cleaned up, the top trimmed and re-hung for longer-term storage. I like to plait the stems to make ropes, again of about 10-12 bulbs. One of these will hang in the kitchen for immediate use, while the remainder are stored in the garage.

Kale

Kale is another winter brassica and very similar to winter cabbage to grow. It is slightly hardier and less susceptible to pests and disease, making it easier still to grow. Its hardiness makes it particularly suitable for growing in cold areas.

The traditional way of raising this crop is to sow seed in a seedbed in April/May, plant out in about July and harvest from November to April (depending on the variety). It will usually require some protection from cabbage whites and from birds and will also need watering in dry weather. However, as a rather tougher, hardier member of the brassica family, you may well find that it is not as attractive to pest species as cabbages or Brussels sprouts. This can be a major advantage to the time-pressed gardener, although unfortunately I find that my family isn't really very keen on it either! When I do grow it I prefer to buy seedlings from a garden centre or by mail order for an August planting, or alternatively to sow seed in later summer or even early autumn. This second option will produce much smaller plants for winter use than does the traditional method, but since this is a leaf crop it doesn't really matter. Small plants can simply be cut whole, rather than the usual habit of picking individual leaves from the more mature plants. With either of these late growing methods the plants are left to their own devices once planted out.

If any plants are still standing in spring the immature flower shoots can be picked and eaten in much the same way as broccoli. Some varieties are better than others for this purpose, Pentland Brig being particularly suitable.

Kohl Rabi

Kohl rabi is a quick maturing crop which, given an adequate water supply, is very easy to produce. It needs to be harvested young while the swollen stems are no larger than a tennis ball. Failure to do so will usually result in these stems becoming woody and stringy. Also, if the water supply is erratic, as it often is in my garden, there is a tendency for the normally spherical stem-balls to split, making them petty much useless. Given this fact and the mild flavour, somewhere between a cabbage and a turnip, which I don't particularly relish, this is not a crop with which I've really persevered. Newer varieties claim resistance to splitting and bolting, which means that low input methods of production are available. For example, given a damp late summer, an August sowing might well lead to good crops in October with very little effort.

Leeks

Leeks are another star of the busy gardener's plot. They are one of the few crops where 'cram in as many as you can fit in and consume' is a good philosophy. The reason for this enthusiasm is their ability to stand in the ground throughout the worst of the winter weather and hence they can be ready for use pretty much continuously from October to March and even into April with a bit of luck. They grow slowly, but will continue to grow through the winter whenever a mild spell of weather occurs. Thus harvesting can be by a process of continually lifting the largest available. Another bonus from the grower's point of view is their relative ease of cultivation; they may be a little bit of a fiddle early on in the production process, but once things are properly underway they can be left to their own devices. Routine weeding and occasional watering in summer dry spells are still beneficial, but the workload really is very light. Leeks are currently the only crop that I bother sowing in a seed bed and then lift and plant out into new positions.

When I first attempted to grow leeks the results were very disappointing. Many were thin and scrawny and others didn't even make it through to the planned winter harvest. At that point I wasn't in the habit of planning my growing in any detail. I tended to fill up my ground as rapidly as possible in early spring and then stick in later crops as soon as space became available. My habit was to buy bunches of bare-rooting leek seedlings from the garden centre in July and to plant them as soon as I had a space, usually after the early potatoes were harvested. It wasn't until I started growing my own leeks from seed and transplanting them that I noticed a radical improvement. My technique now is simply to sow a packet of leek seed in a single drill about 5 metres long across my plot, spacing the seed as evenly as possible, at some point in March. By June a tightly packed row of seedling leeks is growing away strongly. I then remove the best of these, many now as thick as a pencil, and plant them immediately in prepared holes in a new bed, puddling them in. If the day is warm I lift the seedlings into a bucket of water to prevent drying out, and only lift the number I can plant in half an hour or so. I trim the leaves but not the roots of the seedlings before planting. Looking back, I can only assume that the garden centre seedlings I used to buy had been damaged by being out of the ground too long, or were simply too small and weak to survive the ordeal of transplanting.

One of the good points about this crop is that although it is a slow grower, occupying the ground for close to 12 months, the area occupied for the busy spring season is very small. Seedlings sufficient for the whole crop can be grown on a strip 0.5 x 5 metres. Only when these come to be planted out will they occupy a larger area and at this point land starts to become available again as spring crops are harvested. I still put the first double row of leeks into the land vacated by the first early potatoes and the second double row goes in after the (first crop of) broad beans. In our Basic Plan leeks could easily replace some of our over-wintering onions, if some of the preceding potatoes are cleared early enough.

Working in the way described above, I generate 2 staggered double rows of leeks in their final positions, with individuals around 20cm apart in both directions. Closer spacing is possible, but it tends to reduce the average size produced. Overall the technique should provide around 80-100 reasonable sized leeks. If you want to provide much more than this I would suggest growing 2 different varieties. I always go for a very hardy, late maturing variety (e.g. Musselborough), since I don't really want to start harvesting until December, but would like the leeks to survive in the ground until the end of March. This type of selection could be complemented by a much earlier variety (e.g. Pandora) to enable the harvest to start in September. This would not be particularly difficult to achieve, but personally I'd rather eat other things in September, safe in the knowledge that I've got 4 months worth of leeks gradually swelling in the ground.

Lettuce

This, the archetypal salad crop, comes in a huge range of varieties covering a spread of colours, shapes, structures and sizes. Most are really easy to grow, given adequate water and light. However, all, as far as I'm aware, are very susceptible to slug and snail damage, particularly in the cool, damp conditions that predominate at the start of the growing season. They are also, with very few exceptions, a crop that is best eaten within hours of picking. They therefore make most sense for the gardener who has a vegetable patch in the back garden and can nip out to cut a lettuce for tea. They are perhaps of less value to the holder of a distant allotment who has to travel several miles to make a weekly visit.

When it comes to techniques to avoid the worst of the pest problems I would suggest raising seedlings initially indoors and then in a secure area outdoors, but close to the house. Some of these seedlings can be planted out into the plot once they are well established and others can be potted on and remain as pot grown plants. I try to wait for warm, dry weather before putting lettuces into the main plot so that they grow away quickly and survive the inevitable slug assaults.

Onions

Onions are an ideal low maintenance crop. They can be grown from either seed or sets (tiny bulbs). Growing from seed is not particularly difficult and is clearly a cheaper option that using sets, but as saving time is the main issue I always opt for sets. Normally I grow two crops from onion sets per year, one planted in March to mature in August and one planted in September to crop in late June or early July. Specific sets need to be bought for each planting, the second type being known as over-wintering or sometimes Japanese onions.

Onions are virtually a 'plant and forget' crop. I generally hoc quickly down the rows of developing onions a few times during their growing season and will attempt to water them during any prolonged droughts. If forced to rely purely on rainfall the crop will survive, but the yield at the end of a dry season will be much lower than might otherwise be achieved. I would therefore recommend applying an organic mulch around the developing onions in late spring or early summer. I find it best to make sure the crop is well established first before applying a mulch of cut grass or compost, as this can provide encouragement for slugs and snails. If the crop is already growing well it will generally shrug off increased attention from predators, but if conditions are still cold and growth is slow these pests can decimate the tiny plants. Obviously, mulch needs to be put down when the ground is wet to trap the moisture, so it either has to be done as a result of a guess (surely we must be due for some dry weather by now!), or if this point has been missed, then after a one-off heavy watering.

When planting onion sets in either autumn or spring I would always use a wider spacing than is recommended on the packets or in many gardening books. This will make it easier to get the hoe round the developing onions (before mulching!), easier to put down a mulch and should result in bigger onions. I go for about 20cm between sets and 40-50 between rows, but as I've said before these are estimates and I don't waste a lot of time with precise measurements.

Using this approach I expect to start using green onions (i.e. plants which are bulbing up, but which still have a lot of green top growth) from early June. The main harvest of the over-wintered onions follows about a month later. If the ground is wet these need to be lifted and kept somewhere dry to prevent them rotting but if, as is more usual at this time of year, the weather is hot and dry there is no great rush. If properly dried off and stored these early onions should keep until September or October. The harvest of the spring-planted bulbs will follow in August. It's important to get these onions properly dried off, preferably in the sun. With this treatment they should store until the following spring, if they haven't been consumed by then. The timing of the later onion harvest isn't usually too critical, providing conditions are reasonably dry, so it can be fitted in around other jobs.

Parsnips

Parsnips are another really easy crop to grow, although not one of which most of us need vast quantities. The best and largest roots are produced as the result of a long growing season and plenty of water. However, I find that the tradition of sowing them very early in spring just adds to the work and a February sowing, even in the relatively mild West Country climate, gives at best patchy germination requiring a second attempt later on. As a result I don't bother sowing until late March or April. I have even gone to the trouble of sowing in modules and then planting out to provide a good row of evenly spaced plants, rather than the gaps and bunching which can result from direct sowing. The roots may have been slightly smaller and more stumpy when produced this way, but there's no wasted effort in thinning and weeding is easier. Also, giving each plant the space it needs from the start gives them all the chance to reach a decent size.

Once the crop has been planted it gets very little further attention until harvest time. If the season is particularly dry I will attempt to water where I can, particularly early on while the plants are getting established. Weeding is also only necessary while the plants are small. After that they will easily out-compete the weeds.

One of the great things about this crop for busy people is that once it is mature it can be left in the ground without coming to any real harm until it is required in the kitchen. I rarely start harvesting them much before Christmas and would expect to lift the last ones in March, almost a year after sowing. This lengthy occupation of the earth can be seen as a downside to growing parsnips, but as most of us don't grow huge quantities I can't see it as much of an issue. Also, parsnip seed is not the easiest to germinate. It's best to invest in new seeds each year as seed in opened packets rapidly loses its vitality.

Peas

Peas can be a difficult crop to produce in a truly effective and time efficient manner. The challenges include the protection of the young plants against birds and slugs, the provision of supports for the plants, the avoidance of pea moth and the fact that the ripe crop deteriorates rapidly if not picked immediately. I also sometimes feel that peas use a lot of space and effort for a small return on the plate. All of these factors conspire to make peas quite a time consuming crop.

Many gardening books and TV programmes recommend growing a succession of pea crops during the season, with each providing just a single picking. This relies on modern varieties and is to my mind far too much work. Doing all that protection and staking several times over is just not on. I like having home grown peas and regard them as one of the luxuries of the home garden, but this mirroring of commercial production cannot be the way forward for the home producer. Instead, I would suggest growing a tall, vigorous variety which is capable of cropping over a protracted period. I've had success with a variety simply called Victorian Climbing Pea, which can grow to 2.5-3 metres. This clearly needs more effort to support it than a low growing variety, but it is more vigorous, out growing the attention of the pests. It also produced a very much heavier crop over an extended period.

Also, interestingly, these old fashioned varieties will cope better with a slightly haphazard harvesting regime. If picking is missed one week and a batch of pods are left to become over mature once they are removed, the plants will frequently produce more. This doesn't work with more modern varieties bred to produce a single crop.

I'm particularly fond of mange tout peas as they sometimes appear to provide better value on the plate. I like the variety called Carouby de Mausanne. This is also a vigorous plant, growing to about 1.5 metres, with purple flowers and pods which remain tender even when slightly on the mature side, enabling me to pick at my convenience.

Some growers like to start the season off with an over-wintered crop of peas. Personally I've lost too many of the plants to predators of one kind or another to regard this as realistic.

Peppers – Sweet & Hot

To my knowledge, all peppers require a long, warm growing season and therefore growing them outside in the UK is something of a lottery. A warm, sheltered location may give a modest crop some years, but to my mind the likelihood of success isn't really high enough to be worth the effort. They do, however, make a good polytunnel or greenhouse crop. If the tunnel is unheated the best plan is to start the seedlings off on a windowsill in a centrally heated house and only to plant out when the conditions in the tunnel are reliably warm. The root systems of pepper plants are quite small so they can manage in pots for quite some time.

It may be worth considering growing a few plants solely indoors. Given space on a convenient windowsill or conservatory table, the effort involved in watering and feeding a couple of plants is not too great. I did once raise peppers in a pot on my desk at work, in the days when I had an office with natural daylight! If you are going for the indoors approach it may be worthwhile going for chillies rather than sweet peppers as a couple of plants can provide enough chillies to last throughout the year (the small ones dry easily), whereas the yield of sweet peppers will be gone in a couple of meals. It should be remembered that pepper plants are, in fact, perennials and so it is possible to keep them going from one year to the next. This may be more fiddly than they are worth, but a one year old plant will come into fruiting much earlier in the year than one which has been grown from seed that same year.

Potatoes

A number of writers have suggested that the only potatoes worth bothering with are new ones, presumably grown as first earlies, grown quickly and at the start of the season. Their logic is that main crop potatoes take up too much space for most of us land-deprived home growers to contemplate and recognise the fact that potatoes can be purchased cheaply throughout the year and so do not constitute good value from the land they require. I would challenge this view on several grounds. Firstly, my objective is to be as self-reliant as possible within the constraints of time and growing space available; growing my own is more a philosophy in its own right than a simple economic equation. Growing my own means taking control over all inputs into my food regime, guaranteeing the safety and quality of all my produce, managing the environment in which it is produced and the elimination of food miles. On the subject of potatoes specifically, they represent what is probably the only practical large-scale carbohydrate source that is available to the UK home grower. To fail to produce this crop on a significant scale would, from my perspective, leave too great a hole in my home-produced diet that would inevitably end up being filled by commercial sources. Having said all this, if I had to contend with very serious space restrictions then I too would concentrate my efforts on early potatoes. However, given the ease and flexibility of this vegetable, I can't conceive of giving up on main crop/second early potatoes altogether.

One further reason why large-scale potato crops should be included in the cropping plan, particularly in the early years, is their use in gaining control of the land. Rough ground that has been dug, but not totally cleaned of weeds, can be planted with potatoes (preferably second earlies or early main crop) and most annual weeds will be smothered. Furthermore, the action of digging to plant and then to harvest gives excellent opportunities to remove the last vestiges of troublesome perennial weeds. To my knowledge there is no other crop that is so useful in helping growers to gain control of their land.

Early Potatoes

Early potatoes are simply varieties bred to produce a quick crop, usually in around 90 days from planting, given reasonable growing conditions. They could be grown at any point in the growing season, but the seed potatoes are usually only available from January to April, and self-stored tubers are difficult to keep in good condition for much longer than this. The yield produced is smaller than that of an equivalent later/longer season potato, but they have a number of advantages other than the obvious one of getting your hands on a quick crop. The speed of production usually tends to be rapid enough to beat most of the main pests and diseases that can ruin later crops. In particular, earlies can be safely harvested before potato blight strikes and from my experience slug damage is usually minimal, even where the slug population is known to be high. On the downside, early potatoes do not store well; they are grown to be dug and cooked within hours, not days, and so long as they are they provide a welcome treat, regardless of variety.

In view of these factors, if your priority is to get your hands on some home grown potatoes as early possible in the season, then first earlies will be well worth the trouble, but if time is really short I would be inclined to keep things simple and wait for the greater yields on offer from the second earlies. If you are determined to grow really early potatoes it may be worth planting them under a plastic sheet, constructed like a tent, in mid-February. This is clearly an extra hassle, but at least February isn't a particularly busy time in the garden. I've found it will give me a small but useful crop of new potatoes as early as mid-May.

Second Earlies

Second earlies generally take around 100 days to produce a worthwhile crop and will store much better than first earlies, although not as well as main crop potatoes. I have found stored second earlies to be perfectly acceptable as late as the beginning of December, but by New Year they were too badly sprouted to be of much use. As might be expected, yields are generally much higher than with first earlies, but not usually quite as high as main crop potatoes.

Given the moderately short growing season a crop planted from well chitted tubers during the third or fourth week in March can start to be harvested in early July, when the first earlies are coming to an end. This also works well from a pest and disease avoidance point of view. Blight, that great scourge of potato growers, rarely strikes until August and even slugs don't appear to do too much damage if potatoes are lifted in July. This benefit of early potatoes can be accentuated by careful selection of varieties. A few second earlies offer some blight resistance (e.g. Ramano) and some varieties offer good slug and/or eelworm resistance. My favourite slug resistant variety is Kestrel which, although a second early, I have successfully harvested from sluggy ground, as late as the first week in September, with only around 10% of tubers damaged. This wasn't the plan, but I ran out of time!

Given the intermediate nature of second earlies, they can either be used directly from the ground, like firsts, or be dug as a whole crop and stored. In a hot summer I would choose to lift them as they are needed, as suitable cool storage can be hard to find in July and August. If any remain in September, only then would I look to lift and store them as the weather cools.

Main Crop Potatoes

As implied earlier, main crop potatoes offer the highest yields and the longest storage of all potatoes. But, as always, there is a downside: their longer growing season (120 + days) leads to them being the most susceptible to pests and disease. There is no reason why they can't be started off at the same time as the second earlies, but they will require around an extra month in the ground, with some varieties benefiting from even longer. These are often designated as being Late Main Crop and are regarded as needing around a 140 day growing season.

In an ideal world one would want to grow enough main crop potatoes to last from when the second earlies run out, probably in late autumn or early winter, to when the first of next year's first earlies are ready next May. This is a demanding task, the success of which will depend on several factors including the land available, the selection of varieties, the storage facilities to hand and some good luck with the weather! Interestingly, this ambitious target is not really influenced by the time available; potatoes really don't take much effort. The time consuming element is getting enough land into production to enable this quantity of potatoes to be grown, bearing in mind the needs of crop rotation which compels us to have potatoes on no more than about a quarter to a third of the land at any one time. For most of us, though, a gap between the end of the stored old potatoes and the beginning of the new season is probably inevitable. The task is to keep it as short as possible.

As an organic grower I depend on the selection of the correct varieties as my principle defence against the numerous potato problems. Varieties have been developed to be resistant to slugs, potato blight, eelworm, scab and blackleg. Very few, if any, are resistant to all of these problems and so growers must select the varieties most likely to meet their needs. The importance of obtaining undamaged, disease free main crop potatoes cannot be overstated, since the whole purpose of this crop is to store it to provide winter food. Damaged and diseased tubers will not only rot themselves but will spread rot to otherwise perfect tubers. It is therefore well worth sacrificing something in the way of initial yield in order to obtain a high percentage of perfect tubers. One particularly exciting development in recent years has been the development of the Sarpo strain which appears to offer an unprecedented level of blight resistance, as well as high yields and good storage. I grew Sarpo Mira during the very wet, blight ridden season of 2007 and was, I believe, the only person on my allotments to produce a decent potato crop that year.

One other variety of main crop also worth a specific mention is Pink Fir Apple. This old variety with its distinctive, knobbly tubers makes an excellent salad potato and retains its new potato flavour even after months of storage. It tends to produce its tubers in rings around the stem close to the surface, so care is needed if you earth-up. It is a late main crop needing, within reason, as long a season as you can give it, but its excellent flavour and good storage make it worth the effort.

Most writers insist that all potatoes should be earthed up as they grow. This can provide some protection from late frosts and does increase yields. I suspect they are correct, but the increase isn't as great as you might be led to assume. I've grown many perfectly successful potato crops on the 'plant and forget' basis. If late frosts are a particular problem in your area the solution simply has to be to plant a bit later. If large quantities of potatoes are to be grown it's important that they more or less look after themselves, while the gardener gets on with tending to some of the more demanding crops.

Spinach

Spinach is an easy crop to produce, but it can be difficult or time consuming to use it efficiently. Although easily grown, traditional varieties tend to bolt or otherwise deteriorate if left to stand in the plot waiting to be harvested. The advice for growing these varieties is usually to sow small quantities on numerous occasions and to select different varieties for different seasons, e.g. cold tolerant varieties in spring and autumn and drought tolerant ones for summer use. All this is too much hassle for me. Although some of the more modern varieties of spinach (e.g. Matador) claim to be slow to bolt, I tend to avoid the family altogether. Instead, I grow members of the leaf beat/chard/perpetual spinach family. These unrelated crops have a similar use in the kitchen, but I find them much more tolerant of the kind of abuse they have to suffer in my garden.

Squashes

Every year that goes by seems to bring more and more varieties of this intriguing family of vegetables to our seed catalogues. They are not difficult or time consuming to grow, given a sheltered start, fertile ground and plenty of water and it is therefore quite easy to produce a very large weight of orangish, semi-globular fruits. However, the value of these to the self-sufficient can often be rather mixed. A crop only has value in as far as it can be eaten and enjoyed, but many of the largest members of the squash family are, to my taste, rather bland and uninspiring. This is obviously a matter of personal taste, but I would certainly recommend experimentation in the kitchen using a number of varieties before committing too much time, effort and space to their production.

Timing is crucial if this crop, like the other cucurbits, is to be grown. Their tender nature means that seedlings should be raised indoors, hardened off and planted out in the final growing positions. If this is to go smoothly it needs to happen without checking the growth of the plants. It may be that you cannot be certain of the necessary, reliably warm weather and hopefully moist soil in your area before the start of June. Therefore, working back from this date, seeds will probably need to be sown in early May. To get it wrong and do everything too early will only result in time wasted trying to protect the plants, or having lost them to frost/pests, having to start again. Having got the plants off to a good start, they will appreciate water in dry weather, but there is little else to do until harvest.

The other big issue with most members of this family is that they take up a very large area and occupy it for the best part of the growing season. Most squashes grow on large, sprawling plants requiring at least 1 square metre each and may, if the grower isn't careful, produce just one huge, watery fruit. I don't regard this as getting good value from the land I've worked hard for and would therefore suggest growing one of the more compact varieties, perhaps Cream of the Crop or Bon Bon. I also believe that large fruit tend to be very wasteful; it can be difficult to make use of a 10kg of squash at any one time, but 10 individual 1kg fruits are much more useful. Therefore, varieties that produce a large number of smaller fruit are usually preferable, particularly if these fruit store well. Squashes like Butternut and Uchiki Kuri do fall into this category. However, it must be the flavour and hence the overall usefulness of the fruit that give one variety the edge over another, a choice which will come down to personal taste. It is clearly possible to grow a number of varieties together, space permitting, but this can be fiddly and adds to the cost of seeds. Also, extreme care will be needed if attempting to save seed for next season, where several varieties are grown together. Saving seed from squashes is not in itself a difficult exercise, but squashes are notoriously promiscuous and will cross-pollinate given half a chance, so the next generation will not come true and will usually disappoint.

One further angle on squashes as a crop is growing them to eat the seeds, which can be excellent eaten either raw or roasted. Most squash seeds have a hard outer shell with a softer, edible centre. The difficulty is usually removing the outer shell. The easiest way around this problem is to grow a shell-less variety like Lady Godiva (so named because of the naked seeds!).The flesh of this particular squash isn't as flavoursome as many, but its medium sized fruit with yellow and green stripes will pass as acceptable Halloween lanterns once the seeds have been removed, thus entertaining the children while still gaining a useful crop.

Sweetcorn

Sweetcorn really is an easy and very popular crop to produce, so much so that I included it in the Basic Plan. Although it is possible to sow the seeds directly in their growing positions it is not a practice I would recommend as it's likely to result in too many gaps in the patch. If I raise seedlings indoors, harden them off and then plant out in mid to late May I rarely lose a plant. Once planted out and watered in they really can be left to their own devices until harvest, surviving drought better than any other crop I've tried. In the Basic Plan I plant out up to half a bed each year, giving an area of 2.5 x 3 metres. At half metre spacings in both directions this allows for a block of 30 plants. We are advised that pollination is better with this wind pollinated plant if it is grown in a block rather than a single row, and I've certainly not had any problems in this area.

Sweetcorn is the type of crop that produces a relatively small harvest (maybe 40 cobs from our 30 plants), but requires a large space and a huge quantity of plant growth. This is possibly a good thing if you are the sort of busy gardener who is struggling to keep control of a large plot, as this crop is trouble free and rapidly shades out the weeds. However, it can be frustrating to have so much land (up to a sixth of the total growing area in the Basic Plan) committed in this way. Some growers will want to reduce the sweetcorn area as expertise, experience and possibly time available increase.

The only problem I have had with sweetcorn is that it's rather too popular with the larger animals of the area and both deer and badgers come to my rural allotment to gorge on the ripening cobs and flatten the plants in the process.

Swedes

Swedes are another easy crop to produce, although not one I find particularly exciting. They are best sown directly in their growing positions and thinned out as necessary. Provided adequate water is available they don't usually present any problems. Some modern seed varieties provide the option of an early crop. This, to me, appears a particularly pointless exercise. I want Swedes to add a little variety to winter meals when there's not much else in the garden and don't want them appearing while I'm still eating the tomatoes and courgettes of summer. I go for the opposite extreme and pick a variety which is particularly hardy (e.g. Ruby), so that I can leave them in the ground and only harvest as required in the kitchen. This saves both time and storage space.

Tomatoes

If they are grown using the methods favoured by most of our compatriots, tomatoes would not justify a mention in this book. Many British gardeners lavish more time pampering, trimming out side shoots, tying up, watering and feeding their tomatoes than they do on any other crop. No doubt this can produce excellent tomato crops, but it's certainly not the only way.

The extra work generated by this crop comes from two main sources; forcing the plant to grow as a cordon (a single, unbranched stem) when it doesn't really want to and growing them indoors and/or in pots or grow bags, which force the grower into providing all the water and most of the nutrients the plants need. Eliminate these and the work is reduced. It is possible to take a standard tomato variety and allow it to simply do its own thing and take on whatever form it chooses. I've found this to be fairly unsatisfactory, with large sprawling plants, easily broken side branches, muddy and damaged fruit and low yields. It's far better to select a bush variety (also known as determinate rather than the indeterminate cordon varieties – apparently it's due to their ability to produce flowers on their terminal buds rather than just on side shoots). These will naturally form a dome shaped bush and avoid the need for any staking, tying up or removal of side shoots. I like to put a thick mulch of straw around the central stem before the plant gets too big. The branches will then rest on this and the fruit will remain clean and relatively free from damage from slugs and other ground-living pests. If the ground is prepared well before planting with lots of manure or garden compost it's possible to produce respectable crops with no additional feeding at all. I've also found that working this way I can get away with the intermittent watering regime I specialise in. During dry spells each plant will get 5-10 litres of water during my weekly visit to the plot, depending on what water I've got available.

My two favourite varieties for growing this way are Whippersnapper, a small pinkish-red plum tomato which matures early on small plants and Broad Ripple Yellow Current, which produces huge quantities of tiny yellow tomatoes on enormous sprawling plants. Broad ripple yellow current really is a most remarkable plant; initially it can look quite puny but it grows at a tremendous rate to produce bushes over 2 metres across and will keep on fruiting until cut down by autumn frosts. In fact, if the protection of a little fleece is provided in September and the autumn is relatively mild, there's no reason why I can't be still eating these little yellow fruits in November.

Both of these varieties were obtained from the Henry Doubleday Research Association (now known as Grow Organic - www.groworganic. org) and are not, as far as I'm aware, commercially available. However,

I can see no reason why any other bush tomatoes should not be cultivated in the same way. The Real Seed Catalogue (www.realseeds. co.uk) has some promising options. It's interesting to note that most bush tomatoes appear to produce large numbers of small fruit. This isn't a bad thing from our point of view since it enables a few to be lost through splitting (caused by our irregular watering practices) without it making any real difference to the viability of the crop as a whole.

Turnips

Turnips are not a crop I usually bother with. It's not that they are particularly difficult, more that no one in my family is particularly inclined to eat them They are a short season summer crop which doesn't really store well into the winter and, as such, I can find many other things I'd rather give the time and space to. From my experiences of growing them I would suggest sowing a short row on a number of occasions when space is available, and harvesting when still small and tender. No matter how much you may like them, turnips are not a crop of which you will want a whole plot full to mature together. They are probably best grown as an autumn crop, sown after other crops have been cleared in mid to late summer.

Chapter Six
The Home Patch

The Basic Plan we started with in Chapter 2 was based on the idea that the land available to us for growing wasn't on our doorsteps and that this therefore exacerbated the problems facing a time-pressed gardener. It was presented this way in part to deal with the common situation of the new grower with a modern, suburban garden, but without room to commit to a sizeable vegetable patch, who would therefore need to look for an allotment, and in part simply to deal with the worst case scenario. If you are in the fortunate position of being able to do all your growing at home then there's no reason why you can't start in the same way, but it will just become easier to commit the suggested hour or so each week. However, if this is the case you may well wish to move fairly quickly on to at least some of the crops that need more attention. There is a range of crops that are not particularly time consuming, but which need harvesting every few days if the produce is to be at its best (e.g. peas, courgettes, French beans and leaf salad crops). This is a real nuisance for the one hour a week allotment gardener as they are excellent crops, but they are more the preserve of the 10 minutes a day home farmer.

Most of us, however, are not in the fortunate position of having a back garden large enough for all our growing needs, but this need not matter too much. Very successful systems can be created if a small, productive area can be set up at home in combination with a larger, more remote one. This zoning, as it's sometimes called, fits in very well with running our Basic Plan (or variations on it) on an allotment, plus growing a smaller quantity of more demanding crops at home. True, it may be difficult to stick to a rigid, one hour a week time commitment when attempting to do this, but providing the home part of the plan is kept modest, a quick 10 minutes 2 or 3 times a week, perhaps on returning from work, should suffice.

A further benefit of the dual plot system is that the home plot can be an invaluable asset in producing seedlings to plant out on the main plot. At the start of the season I have an area for hardening off plants raised indoors (pumpkins, beans and sweetcorn etc.) before they are planted out. Later I use the same area to sow winter and spring brassicas in modules to plant out after the over-wintered onions have been lifted on the allotment. I've found these small plants to be particularly vulnerable to slug attack while in their pots and modules if left on the ground. To avoid this problem I use an old patio table as my hardening off/outdoor sowing area to keep the plants above the pest level. To be sure of complete safety I immerse each leg of the table in a plastic tub (ice cream or margarine) of water. This is the patio table growing area referred to a number of times in earlier chapters (see photograph). If I have time I also use this protected area to raise salad leaves and herbs in pots. These salads never get planted out but are cut directly from the pots. Grown this way they are not only free from pest damage, but also clean from soil splash.

The challenge with any pot/container based growing system is keeping the plants watered and fed. To deal with the easy bit first, I do not keep any productive plants in pots for an extended period: before they've exhausted the nutrient in the multipurpose potting compost they were sown in, or potted up into, it's time to plant them out, or eat them in the case of salads on the table. Thus there is no feeding of my plants in pots. Watering, on the other hand, is not so easily dealt with. In hot, dry weather the plants on the table will need watering every day and, even if cooler but still dry, 3 days is about the absolute limit between waterings. This can be a major imposition for our type of gardener; it's not the 5-10 minutes spent watering, it's the fact that it has to be a daily event that's the problem. The only answer is to bear this in mind from the start and keep the number of plants involved down to what is really needed, and keeping them in one location (the table) also helps. I use the growing table mainly to prepare seedlings at the start of the season when temperatures are not so high and some rainfall in common. If you don't expect to be able to water plants pretty much every day in June and July, make sure the table is empty by then.

In addition to the table top nursery, the home plot can also include a seed bed to produce bare-rooted seedlings for the main plot. Leeks and brassicas are frequently grown in this way and having the seed bed to hand makes it easier to take better care of the small plants. Growing them directly in the soil means they will need much less watering than if they were in pots. Onions too could be raised from seed in this way, but personally I don't bother as it's quicker to buy sets than to raise my own from seed.

Another useful addition to the home plot is a cold frame or two. These provide ideal conditions for raising and hardening off seedlings for use elsewhere, at the start of the season. Having an intermediate growing area between the over warm house and the often over cool garden table is very useful and makes the production of good, strong seedlings that much easier. Once this role is nearing completion cold frames can also be used to start off a few of the more tender crops (e.g. courgettes, tomatoes or even melons). These crops can be planted in the cold frame roughly a month earlier than they would be in the open garden, safe in the knowledge that frost protection is provided, thus enabling a longer growing season with the potential of larger crops over a longer period. If timed correctly (this may need a little experimentation), the plants will be just pushing against the lid of the cold frame when the weather has warmed up and frosts are past and so the lids can be removed. At the other end of the season a range of crops (particularly salads, short season carrots, Chinese greens etc.) can be sown in the cold frame with the lid off as late as August, and then the lid replaced over the now thriving crop in about October. The crops can then be harvested as required over the winter.

The challenge once again, with this addition to the system, is time. Cold frames need daily or even twice daily attention during the key spring season and again in the autumn, if in use. Ventilation is needed on warm days, but lids must be shut and even extra insulation added on cold nights, and time is also required, as ever, for watering. If you are the type of gardener who is happy to adopt a regular routine of checking the frames every morning and evening, say either side of the day job, this approach to gardening has much to offer. The total time commitment is not great and it does offer the prospect of getting your own healthy food over a longer season as well as significantly increasing production from a small space. However, if you are running an allotment as well as the home patch, as well as everything else in a busy life, it may be one step too far. For those for whom the idea of gardening under protection appeals, it may be worth taking things one stage further and going for a greenhouse or polytunnel.

Growing Under Protection

The benefits of growing crops completely under protection are fairly obvious: protection from adverse weather conditions accelerates plant growth and enables useful production at times of the year which would otherwise be impossible. It also enables the production of crops that are too tender to be reliable in the open garden. The technique can also enable us to make better use of the land available by cropping it productively for more, if not all, of the year.

However, all this brings with it a further set of challenges to the time-starved gardener. The increased growing temperatures and protection from the elements provided by a greenhouse or polytunnel mean that the plants have a greatly increased demand for water: a demand which has to be satisfied by the gardener alone. In warm weather a typical greenhouse or polytunnel will need a thorough watering every day. It will also need attention to adjust ventilation, not to mention the need to pick the ready supply of produce generated by the enhanced growing conditions. For these reasons I believe even a modest greenhouse or polytunnel is not a sensible addition to the complete outdoor growing systems explored here (i.e. the remote/allotment plot, plus the outdoor home patch); there simply isn't time for everything. One could be included and used in much the same way as a cold frame, but I'm not convinced that the limited utilisation would justify the trouble and expense. It is as an alternative to part, or even to all, of the outdoor growing systems that polytunnels and greenhouses are proposed for the busy grower.

The medium to large greenhouse or polytunnel is ideal for the back garden grower who wants to do the majority of his/her gardening under cover. It makes particular sense if the growing space is very restricted, as well as time, to grow under cover and so make maximum use of what land is available. It enables crops to be produced more quickly, the growing season to be lengthened and the number of annual crops from the same land increased. I would suggest that growing under cover is particularly applicable to the back garden gardener rather than the allotment grower, as the tunnel or house will need daily, if frequently brief, attention. Judging by my own standards, I know this won't happen if travelling is required. Also, the large volume of water needed will probably be easier to provide at home.

Greenhouse or Polytunnel?

The decision on which to go for comes down to personal circumstances and taste, but in case there's any doubt some of the key factors are listed below:

- Polytunnels give much more growing space for the price
- Greenhouses are more robust and last longer
- Polytunnels are quicker and easier to put up
- Greenhouses are generally more attractive
- Greenhouses are easier to heat in winter, if this is part of the plan

In the end the price is usually the deciding factor, particularly if you want to create a large, covered growing area. Many householders will regard a modest 2 x 3 metre garden greenhouse as affordable, but when it comes to the larger sizes (4 x 10 metres), a polytunnel may still be acceptable but the greenhouse would be prohibitively expensive. The cost per square metre of polytunnel growing space falls dramatically as the size of the tunnel increases.

The question of how to make the best and most time effective use of a newly created under cover growing area is a complex one, and one which comes down to personal preferences as much as it does to horticultural techniques. The following thoughts are not meant to be either prescriptive or exhaustive, but are designed to set the thought processes into action and to give a starting point to debate regarding this most exciting area of home food production.

I know quite a few home farmers who simply use their greenhouses to raise seedlings for planting out in the main garden in the spring, and then to grow tomatoes in the summer. Whilst there is nothing wrong with this approach it strikes me as rather a shame not to make more use of this excellent growing environment. In general terms it is possible to grow most of the crops you can grow outside under either plastic or glass about a month earlier than can be done outside. There is, therefore, a huge opportunity to start off hardy crops in late winter or very early spring and harvest them before the summer crops are planted out. At the other end of the season, it is relatively easy to plant crops in mid to later summer for harvesting in late autumn or the early part of the winter. Over-wintered crops too will benefit from the lengthened season and be ready very much earlier and usually in better condition than if they were outside.

The main factors that govern what is grown are the space available under cover and the time the gardener has to work on the crops. Many gardeners who have recently bought a greenhouse or polytunnel are on record as saying that they wish they'd bought something a bit bigger, because once they've started growing this way, more and more ideas become apparent. So the message on size might be as follows; if in doubt go for the larger size! On the time front I would suggest handling things at a steady pace throughout the year, with a succession of small crops spread out, rather than a summer glut. This is best achieved by setting up a bed system similar to our outdoor plot, and then planning in advance what will follow what in each of the beds. All the same rules about crop rotations and sustainability apply both inside and out, it's just that gardening under cover is that bit more intensive. With care it should be possible to be harvesting something from the under cover garden throughout the year. Nothing will actually grow in an unheated greenhouse or polytunnel when the temperature is below 5°C, but many hardy plants will survive quite happily, growing steadily during milder spells and can be harvested as required.

If you make the decision to use a polytunnel or a large greenhouse as part or all of your growing system, remember that all the water that will be needed for growing in that warm environment will have to be provided by you. If you are not careful, this task can overwhelm the busy gardener. As with most things discussed here, the secret is to plan the irrigation from the very start. If you can site the house or tunnel close enough to your own house to simply connect a hose, you will have a workable solution, albeit an expensive one if you are on a water meter! Also, in these environmentally aware times, total reliance on the mains water may not be acceptable in the longer term. Besides, hosepipe bans are common in many parts of the country.

One advantage of greenhouses over polytunnels is that it is much easier to collect water from a greenhouse roof than it is from most polytunnels. However, whatever type of house you go for I would suggest that, with a bit of ingenuity, some sort of rainwater capturing system should be possible. I've also noticed recently that at least one major polytunnel supplier is now offering rain water capture systems. It may not always be practical to rely entirely on rainwater, but it should be possible to capture at least some to supplement the mains supply.

There are also a number of things we can do to minimise the time we spend applying water. Firstly, we need to garden in such a way as to minimise consumption. To me this means keeping the ground covered as much as possible to minimise evaporation. I would use organic mulches around crops and even cover empty ground with polythene to prevent it drying out. We want to ensure that, as far as possible, all the water we struggle to provide is used by the plants, not wasted in evaporation.

There are a range of slow-release or self-watering products now available on the market and designed specifically to reduce the grower's workload. These range from large scale drip irrigation systems that require the pressure of the water mains to drive them, through smaller systems that will work from a water butt, to the simplicity of plastic spikes which fit onto old soft drinks bottles and allow the water to seep out next to selected plants. The time to decide on which of these plethora of products suits your own pocket is at the planning stage, not in mid-summer when your plants are withering in an overly dry house! Once again the secret of success is to plan ahead.

Chapter Seven
Keeping Chickens in the Garden

Given enough space and our desire to make as large a contribution to our collective diets as possible, the idea of keeping poultry requires little debate. So far our efforts in the garden have produced a good range of fruit and vegetables, providing a sizeable proportion of the vitamins, minerals, fibre and carbohydrates which we need, but not really that much in the way of protein. If we are really going to take control of the food we eat we need to grasp this area too. For the vast majority of us this means livestock. At this point we need to be realistic about our diets. I don't believe that a vegan or a purist vegetarian diet is realistic for the ordinary self-sufficient grower living in the UK. Given more time and space, together with a large heated growing area, anything might be possible, but for most of us we can either choose to buy in all our protein (animal or vegetable), or choose to produce what we can ourselves. For me the choice is always to do as much as I can and keeping a small number of hens, principally for their eggs, is the simplest, the least demanding and probably the most entertaining way I can do this.

I've emphasised egg production rather than meat for a number of reasons. The main one is that although I don't have a fundamental problem in killing and eating surplus birds (generally cockerels), it is a somewhat messy and time consuming business and one which I don't particularly like doing. Personally, I have no time for the oft heard "I couldn't eat it if I had to kill it myself", feeling as I do that total involvement in the process or total vegetarianism are not the only two acceptable options. I just don't do it any more often than necessary as using an entire morning killing, plucking, drawing and joining 2-3 cockerels, only to produce one meal for the family, is not how I choose to spend my time. It does, however, make me very grateful for the high quality, ready to eat birds available from my local farm shop. I am grateful in particular for all the hard work that's gone into getting them from the farmyard to my refrigerator. Clearly, if I were to raise birds specifically for their meat, they may be larger or present better value in terms of preparation time, but this is an area I've yet to investigate.

The strength of the argument for producing our own eggs is, if anything, stronger than that for producing our own fruit or vegetables. The subject of battery egg production is well known to all and this is clearly not an industry that most of us would want to support. What is less well known is the relatively small amount of space allocated to birds raised under commercial 'barn' conditions. I wouldn't claim to be an animal welfare expert, but I wouldn't want to provide anything less than the commercial free range standard of 10m^2 per bird. Thus I'm not prepared to consider any of the more enclosed or semi-intensive options open to the domestic poultry keeper. Clearly this presents a problem in terms of the amount of land available, particularly as it will be necessary to move the birds on to fresh land periodically to allow the grass to grow back and prevent the build up of parasites. Chickens will take quite a significant proportion of their diet from the grass and any other plants around them. This is good news from the point of view of keeping the grass under control without having to spend time mowing, but it is a worry because they prefer to feed from our vegetable beds if they get the chance. They will always need to be kept in a designated area away from most other parts of the productive garden. For this reason, as much as for their own protection, we use a portable electric fence.

Combining chicken keeping with fairly intensive food growing on a small plot of land is not always the easiest of objectives as the chickens will, if given the chance, destroy most crops. One combination that does work well is to combine chicken keeping with top fruit growing. Chickens can be kept in an orchard and may actually improve the production since they will eat any pests spending part of their life cycle on the surface soil, in leaf litter or in fallen fruit. They will also feed on fallen fruit which may otherwise go to waste, but the only time hens can be detrimental to fruit trees is when the trees are very young and not properly established. If I want to run poultry in an area containing new fruit trees I have to use a double mulching technique. The trees are first surrounded by a layer of rotten manure to feed them and hold in the water and then a layer of broken bricks, stone, rubble etc. is added. The rubble needs to be in pieces too large for the chickens to move.

Without the rubble the chickens would soon have the manure scattered as part of their relentless search for worms.

If you are in the fortunate position of having a reasonable piece of land close to home for easy access, but no time for most growing systems, you could certainly do a lot worse than plant it up as an orchard and keep chickens beneath the trees.

It may come as a surprise to many that keeping hens for eggs is not only a rewarding pastime but also one which demands very little daily effort. I refer to daily effort quite deliberately as hens will normally require a few minutes each morning to release them from their sleeping quarters and feed them. They then require a little feed again in the afternoon and finally the time it takes to shut them up each evening. This may be little more that 10 minutes per day, but as they are living animals it must be done every single day. It is because of the need to include the poultry in the daily routine that I include them in the home patch options. Some allotment societies still allow the keeping of domestic poultry on their sites, but if twice daily travel is required, then for me the effort would be too much.

One of the great things about keeping these birds is that if you keep a cockerel as well, it is really quite easy to get them to replace themselves. Most hens go broody from time to time and will want to hatch a batch of eggs. Our principle of producing chicks has been to just let them get on with it. A broody hen needs to be provided with separate accommodation and food and water, but producing a new generation of hens this way is neither difficult nor time consuming for the poultry keeper. It will, however, produce as many cockerels as it will hens, or often more, sod's law being what it is! To the non-expert like me it is difficult to tell hens and cocks apart until they exhibit adult plumage and behaviour. For this reason I usually end up killing the young cockerels at around 16-20 weeks of age, when they are at least big enough to offer something worthwhile for the table. This is certainly not a task I relish or one which is a particularly efficient use of my time in getting a meal on the table, but it is a part and parcel of raising new hens.

Chapter Eight
The Fruit Garden

So far our plans have proceded as if vegetables were the only thing that we have any interest in growing, the sole reference to the orchard being as a chickens' playground. This is clearly not the case. Fruit also offers huge scope and interest, without necessarily demanding too much effort from the gardener.

Fruit growing represents the other half of the balanced equation that is the self-sufficient garden. Fruit is a very important part of the diet, providing vital vitamins as well as variety and interest, but it is frequently left to take second place in the productive garden. I can see no good reason for this and consider it worthwhile to commit a sizeable proportion of my available time and space to the production of fruit. In terms of taking control of our diets, ensuring food quality and eliminating food miles, it's important that we look to substitute as much commercial produce with home grown as we can.

Before getting down to specific details there are a few general points regarding fruit production that are particularly relevant to the time-starved gardener:

- The fruit we eat is the fruit of selected perennial plants

- These plants need to be nurtured for at least a year and possibly up to 10 years before good crops can be obtained

- Over the long term fruit growing to reasonable standards is not particularly difficult or time consuming

- To be successful it needs time investment well ahead of the rewards and it needs a stable, fixed location for a number of years

- In general terms, the larger the plant, the more it produces, the longer it takes to get it into production, but less effort (per year) is required over its life cycle.

- To give good returns in proportion to the effort expended a fruit tree/plant needs to be suited to its conditions – principally climate and soil type.

- Growing fruit, when viewed over the long term, can actually be less effort than growing vegetables, although 'pound for pound' comparisons are very difficult.

Getting Started

One very important difference between fruit growing and vegetable growing stems from the fact that the majority of fruit is produced by perennial plants, whereas most vegetables are annuals. It will take a number of seasons to establish a productive fruit garden, whereas a good yield of vegetables can be produced from year one. It is therefore advisable to set about planting fruit at the first possible opportunity, once the ground is clear of weeds. Since most fruit bushes and trees will be in place for many years it obviously makes sense to get the ground into good shape before planting them. It is possible to make improvements after planting, but it is always going to be easier to remove weeds and improve the soil fertility first.

In an ideal world it might make sense to suggest planting up a complete fruit garden as soon as a suitable patch of land is clear, thus minimising the time to the first fruit harvest. However, this is all too much for most of us. Firstly, committing most of the precious cleared land to fruit production will mean no harvest of any kind at the end of the first growing season. Also, fruit bushes and trees can constitute a major expense, which may be best spread over several seasons. I would therefore recommend a gradual approach, under which land is steadily cleared, involving the use of one or more vegetable crops to help the process along (usually potatoes) and then, in a specific area, these vegetable crops can be gradually replaced by fruit. This methodology gives the satisfaction of some produce from the land each season, gives a chance to eradicate perennial weeds and spreads the investment needed for a good fruit garden over several years. I have taken this one stage further by taking on two separate small allotment plots at different times. The first ran the Basic Plan for a few years (or at least a version of it while I was developing the idea). When I took on the second plot I converted the first to soft fruit and perennial vegetables and cleared the second plot to set up the Basic Plan for vegetables. Expanding in this way gave a steadily increasing fruit harvest, building up to a major contribution to our diet without at any point taking on an unsustainable workload or putting up with a year or two without anything to show for my efforts.

Having decided on the general approach and identified the land to be used, the obvious next question is what to grow. In my opinion most fruit is best enjoyed fresh and since most has a limited season, it is best to grow as wide a variety of types as is possible. I would therefore recommend growing most of the commoner soft fruit, plus a range of top fruit and would suggest, where possible, a number of varieties of each to spread the pickings over as wide a season as possible. This can go against our intention of keeping the time invested to a minimum, but picking moderate quantities of fruit is rarely a time consuming activity. Nevertheless, thought is required to ensure that a workable plan is cobbled together from the start.

Decisions need to be based not only on the particular likes and dislikes of your own family, but also on how you would like to use the produce. For example, planning to produce more strawberries than you can possibly eat during a 2 week period in June may be a waste of space and effort for many, but if you intend to produce a year's supply of strawberry jam it becomes the perfect plan. I would not recommend allotting too much space to growing exotic, warmer climate species. Whilst it is perfectly possible to grow peaches and apricots outside in the UK, all such crops are likely to occupy space and time out of all proportion to their actual contribution to your diet. By all means, put a peach tree in a particularly sheltered corner of your garden, but don't commit too much of your valuable time and land to a range of crops that aren't really suited to our climate.

Where to Grow the Fruit?

At first glance this might appear rather a self evident question with the obvious answer, wherever you've got the room! My observation here is that most gardeners appear to view fruit as something they grow at home, if at all, while if they keep an allotment it is reserved for vegetable production. This makes sense if your fruit production is limited to a few small apple trees on the lawn, or a few strawberry plants at the front of an herbaceous border, or indeed any system of mixing the fruit in with an ornamental or recreational garden. However, most fruit production is very well suited to the type of gardening regime that the busy gardener can employ at the allotment, or indeed any similar growing area away from the home. Pretty much all fruit, with the possible exception of strawberries, can be grown with the intermittent attention characteristic of the busy gardener who only gets to the allotment once a week, and even then not always. Fruit trees and bushes can be planted throughout the late autumn and winter to suit the grower, provided the ground isn't frozen and much of the pruning can be done at the same time of year. In the summer it's just a question of keeping any weeds under control, some light pruning and, of course, the harvest. Ideally most fruit should be picked when ripe, but most is quite forgiving about a few days either way. Certain top fruit (particularly some varieties of apples and pears) is grown specifically to ripen in storage after picking and so can be picked more or less at our convenience. The perennial fruit trees and bushes are much tougher than the annual vegetable plants and are, once established, much more able to look after themselves.

I can only assume that fruit growing on allotments is not so common because of the investment required and the fact that the land is not owned by the plot holder. It may also be fear of vandalism that discourages the purchases. Some allotment societies have rules on the use of the land, but I've not heard of any specifically banning fruit production. Irrespective of the rules, though, it's clearly not acceptable to put a 10 metre tall apple or pear tree in a place where it will deny another plot-holder's land the sun it needs. Not that anyone would really want to, as the equivalent trees on dwarfing root stocks are readily available. These can be kept to around 2-3 metres high, making both picking and pruning easier and quicker, without the need to offend the neighbours.

You will notice that my summary of tasks does not include spraying. As an organic and slightly lazy grower this is something I simply don't do. I will always try to avoid problems rather than having to interfere in order to solve them. The best trick is to grow disease resistant varieties wherever possible. Why grow the stereotypical Cox's Orange Pipin which cannot be kept free from pest and disease without lots of chemicals when there are plenty of equally good varieties which are much less hard work. With organic gardening becoming more and more popular the number of resistant varieties in the fruit catalogues increases every year. Also, when checking over the forming fruit in summer, if I find a twig to be diseased or infested with pests, my normal reaction is to cut it off and burn it. It doesn't take many minutes to give a modest fruit garden a quick check over every few weeks of the growing season and this will enable most problems to be nipped in the bud – literally! Overall, I have to admit that yields are probably slightly lower than they would be if employing a rigorous spraying regime, but I haven't got time for one and I wouldn't be happy to employ one anyway.

The following sections contain various ideas on the production of fruit crops with the minimum of effort.

Strawberries

Strawberries are probably the most delicious and therefore the most popular of the soft fruits. They are not difficult to grow, but they probably do need more attention than just about any other fruit crop. Because of the popularity of the fruit and the superior flavour of home grown strawberries over their shop bought counterparts, many growers will feel that the extra effort is well worth it. I wouldn't disagree, but I would comment that I've wasted many pounds of strawberries over the years by growing them on an allotment and not having the time to visit and pick them on a daily basis. If I'd had room to grow them at home and hadn't tried to grow so many other things at the same time, I'd have done much better.

Strawberries are a short-lived, low-growing perennial plant which can be obtained as either young plants in pots or as bare-rooted runners bought in one summer/autumn, and planted out to be productive during the following summer. They are easy to grow and provide a treat which few of us can resist. They are usually sold singly in pots in garden centres, or bare-rooted in 10s by mail order suppliers. For most of us 10 plants of any one variety is probably enough to start with, but it makes sense to have at least two varieties, with different fruiting times to spread the crops. This is, in my view, a classic soft fruit crop that is best eaten within hours of harvesting and which, unless you are a real jam fanatic, or make your own ice-cream, isn't worth attempting to preserve or store. It is tempting, though, to grow a small number of each of a large number of varieties. This makes for an interesting experiment to find which do best under the local conditions, but longer term it can be both time consuming and wasteful to have to harvest just a handful of ripe strawberries at a time. When selecting varieties I will always go for those which offer a resistance to grey mould and mildew. As an organic grower I have no intention of spraying to combat these diseases and need all the help from the plant breeders I can get. New varieties of strawberry are continually appearing on the market. Read the labels carefully and make a selection to obtain a long cropping season, good disease resistance and, above all, a good flavour.

Unsurprisingly, strawberries are popular with a range of pests, including wild birds, slugs and snails, escaped chickens, pet rabbits and visiting children etc. If those of us who have worked to produce them are to get any crop to speak of, it's essential that the plants are netted as soon as the berries start to form. Make sure you have the nets ready in advance. It's also worthwhile mulching under the developing fruit to keep them clear of the ground, free from mud splashes and less accessible to the slugs. Straw, surprisingly enough, is the traditional material for this purpose, but modern large scale growers usually opt for a black, plastic mulch. Using nematodes (a biological control) to reduce the slug population is also worth considering.

Strawberries can be grown very effectively in large pots, grow bags and even hanging baskets. These can all be positioned off the ground and hence the crop will be clean and free from slug damage. These are significant benefits, but it must also be remembered that crops grown in this way need much more watering and feeding than those grown in the ground. Normally I wouldn't recommend growing anything in this way as the extra time involved is significant. However, strawberries are one of those crops which are popular enough to justify the extra effort. If you want to make strawberries a priority for special treatment (and why not?), just make sure that the quantities grown, the location and the conflicting priorities are properly planned so that effort and resources don't end up being wasted. In the past I've wrecked my chances of a nice, early strawberry crop by failing to water the pots and almost killing the plants, but if I hadn't been trying to achieve so many other things at the same time, … who knows?

Strawberry plants will start to decline in their productivity after 3 4 seasons and are probably best removed after the 4th crop and replaced elsewhere in the garden. The ideal solution is to pot on runners produced by the plants during their third season, plant these in a new strawberry bed at the end of the season (on land that has never before grown strawberries) and to dig up the parent plants as they decline after 4 productive years. Because of the relatively short life expectancy of strawberry plants many gardeners prefer to grow them as part of the vegetable plot rather than in with the permanent plantings of the fruit garden. A low effort way of rotating the strawberry plot, which I've seen used (it didn't fit my garden so I haven't yet tried it), is to grow 3 or 4 rows of strawberries and every year to allow the runners from the right hand row to grow out to the right and create an extra row. At the end of the season the left hand row of old plants can be dug up and the strawberry bed is therefore constantly being renewed as it migrates across the vegetable garden.

Blackberries

Blackberries grow on large, rambling vine-like plants which are usually spiny. Numerous modern cultivars exist, most of which have had the thorns bred out and the berry size enhanced. In theory the flavour of such varieties is also better than the wild hedgerow plant. The yield from a single plant can be quite large (up to 10kg) but they are large, spreading plants that take up a lot of space (3-4 metres of fence or trellis). From a time investment point of view, though, they offer good value. An annual regime of: cutting out old or dead wood in autumn, tying in, a spring mulch of manure or compost and, of course, late summer picking is all that is required to give a good crop.

I'm fortunate enough to live in a country area where there are many miles of hedgerow, much of it infested with brambles. As a result I prefer to gather what can be had for free from the countryside, rather than use any of my precious growing land for this crop. True, it would be nice to be able to harvest the berries without having to think about the thorns, but on balance I'm simply not prepared to sacrifice the space. I've also noticed that the wild blackberries with which these isles are blessed exhibit a huge genetic variation (I'm told there are around 400 sub-species). Research and many miles of trekking the public areas and footpaths has revealed prize patches that produce berries of superior size and flavour to their regular cousins and which, in my view at least, are easily as good as the cultivated varieties. I know this is scarcely time efficient, but the dog has to be walked! I'm also careful to only pick the fruit growing well away from roads and intensively farmed fields to avoid contamination.

If you have the luxury of plenty of land or are just determined to grow a thornless variety, it's worth knowing that these plants are very easily propagated at home. The easiest way is by layering, by simply burying the end of a trailing shoot. When new growth is spotted coming up from the earth where the shoot is buried, it's reasonable to assume there will be roots beneath, and the original shoot can be cut and the new plant moved to its new position.

Raspberries

In my view raspberries are worth the space and effort in any productive garden. This may be in part because they are my favourite soft fruit, but I also find that they are much less work than strawberries, with which they compete on flavour, and only marginally more effort that blackberries which are not usually so delicious. The growing regime, once established, is much the same as blackberries, although returns will be greater if some netting is provided to keep birds off the harvest. As regards ease of production they beat strawberries on a number of counts. Firstly, as with all these plants, the biggest job is establishing them in the first place. Raspberries will be productive for at least 10 years, so replacement does not come around very often. Also, being a tall crop compared to strawberries, there is no need to worry about slugs and other ground based pests. I find too that ripe fruit remains in decent condition on the plants for several days, rather than needing the almost daily attention of the strawberry bed.

When establishing a new raspberry bed I plant the new canes out in a single row with wire supports between stout posts, going for a fairly wide planting distance of about 45cm. The ground needs to be fertile (add muck or compost) and free from perennial weeds before starting, as removing the weeds later is virtually impossible. I would also leave plenty of room on either side of the row before planting anything else. Over the years the raspberry canes will put up new shoots up to a metre away from the parent plants. The easiest way of growing this crop is to regard this phenomenon as a bonus and allow the single row to develop into a thick and slightly erratic hedge. Some remotely growing new canes will always have to be dug up and replanted or discarded, but if space for a good wide hedge has been included in your calculations from the start, this can be kept to a minimum.

The normal practice when setting up a raspberry bed is to plant the canes in the winter and cut them back. This encourages strong plant/root growth, but doesn't lead to a crop until the second summer, 18 months later, which is a long time to wait. However, the autumn fruiting varieties (e.g. Autumn Bliss, All Gold) fruit on the current season's growth and can therefore be brought into production less than a year after planting. Recent developments have seen the availability of so-called long stemmed varieties (primo-cane) which have been developed specifically to produce a crop in their first summer. As with all such things you have to pay a premium for these plants from the mail order company, but for me reducing the wait for the first fruit to 6 months made them well worth the extra money, even though the first crop was not large.

One other point to note with summer raspberries is that, because they produce new canes one year which will fruit the next, the gardener always needs to have one eye on next year's potential crop. For example, in a particularly dry season the raspberry canes may fruit well without being watered, but the production of the new growth for next year will be poor. Ideally, in such circumstances the gardener needs to find time for extra watering and mulching. If he/she doesn't, it's likely the plants will recover in the long term, but one year's crop will have been lost or severely curtailed.

Blackcurrants

Given a rich soil and a little protection from the birds at fruiting time, blackcurrants can be a very easy crop to produce using a growing system which borders on neglect. I also find that I can produce much larger currants of greater sweetness and superior flavour than those I find available for sale. Plants will put up with seasonal water-logging and with partial shade, but they will not crop satisfactorily on overly dry or impoverished soil. They can produce up to 3kg of fruit per bush per year and therefore, at a spacing of 1.75-2 metres each way, represent a reasonable return on the space. They will take a good few years to attain this level of cropping, but will continue to produce well for up to 15 years.

Blackcurrants are renowned for being heavy feeders but, given soil which was initially both fairly rich and heavy, mine survive quite well on a load of manure each winter and a good sprinkling of wood ash in the early spring. To minimise both weeding and watering I would recommend mulching the ground beneath the bushes throughout the growing season, or all year round if easier – just part the mulch to feed. Blackcurrants fruit mostly on one year old wood so the pruning regime has to be designed to maximise new growth. The usual way of doing this is to go round the bushes once each winter and cut out the oldest stems at the base. This is not a major chore, but if it's missed one winter the effect on production is only modest.

In most parts of the country wild birds will always take a significant proportion of the crop if it's not protected by netting. In an ideal world we would all grow our soft fruit in a fruit cage, providing permanent protection and easy access for ourselves. These are, however, expensive and time consuming to build so, like most growers, I rely on temporary netting which I move around from one crop to the next as needed. Even if only draped over the bushes I find these a lot better than nothing in the way of bird protection. It is very tempting to pick the currents as soon as they start to ripen, to get in ahead of the birds. However, if you can protect the fruit a bit longer until it is fully ripe I think the improvement in sweetness and flavour is well worth the risk. Given naturally heavy fertile soil, blackcurrants are certainly an excellent low effort crop.

Red and White Currants

Superficially red and white currants may appear very similar to black, but there are some important differences; they are less tolerant of wet growing conditions and they fruit on older wood. This latter difference clearly affects both how they are pruned and the shape of the plant. The effect of the former will be self evident. They will, however, tolerate lack of direct sunlight, although the flavour of the fruit may be affected. Red and white currants are effectively the same species, the red variant being a sport (a freak genetic mutation) from the white and so their requirements are identical.

Red and white currents are probably not the sort of fruit that any of us want in very large quantities; although they look beautiful their usage is limited. This statement may say more about the limits of my imagination, rather than those of the fruit, but I would suggest that a single bush will probably give all the redcurrants most of us might need. If this turns out not to be the case the stock is easily increased by taking cuttings of long (circa 20cm) one year old growth in the autumn and sticking them in the ground to ¾ of their length. By next spring most will have rooted. Blackcurrants can also be propagated by this casual method.

Top Fruit

Top fruit, or tree fruit, is self-evidently fruit grown on trees rather than the shrubs and bushes we've so far discussed. They can take up a lot of space and take a long time to produce decent quantities of fruit, but when they do they can produce quite a lot as a result of very little effort from the gardener. In view of this combination of high production and low effort, I consider that a selection of tree fruit should feature in every productive gardener's plans. However, there is often a trade-off between the work needed to produce the crop and the space required. A big old apple tree takes up a lot of space in the garden and will often produce a large crop of fruit with no input at all from the grower, but more restricted forms of tree may require more effort to keep them productive. Even using smaller trees in controlled forms, though, the annual workload is not that onerous, and much of it can be done to suit the gardener rather than demanding attention 'this weekend'.

The range of top fruit available to the home producer is large and, judging from the catalogues that continually come through my letterbox, ever expanding. Here I have limited discussion to the more common options and areas where I have personal experience. Our objective is to produce as much of our own fruit as we can with as little time commitment as possible, bearing in mind the inevitable constraints of space/land available. I have not considered exotic species that, with a great deal of care and attention, could produce in the UK. Also, as with vegetable growing, the focus is on systems and approaches that specifically help the time-starved gardener. Attention is drawn too to the Further Reading list for more information on the specifics of fruit growing and details of tender crops not covered here.

Apples

Apples are quite rightly the most popular and widely grown top fruit crop in the UK. Varieties can be found that will suit pretty well all lowland growing conditions and there are nurseries specialising in promoting apple varieties adapted to harsher, upland and exposed locations. Notwithstanding the earlier comments about looking after trees grown in restricted forms, significant crops of high quality apples can be produced by the home gardener with very little effort. They will welcome good soils and sheltered positions, but will also cope with less than perfect conditions in both respects.

Having decided to grow apples the next question is your objective; do you want to grow eating apples, cookers or apples for cider production and how much space is available. The range of apple cultivars available is huge (several thousand at least) so it's important to have a clear idea of how you intend to use the fruit from the start. Many older cultivars were developed for use over winter. Apples which only ripened after a few months in storage were invaluable in times past before refrigeration and fruit imports, but they are of limited value to us if we don't have suitable (cool, but frost free) storage areas. With this in mind I would suggest that the potential self-sufficient should be looking to produce a succession of apples which can be eaten from the tree as they ripen from August to November. Some of the last batch can then be stored, but the volume will probably be fairly small and not present too great a problem. To these I would add a couple of cooking apples, giving a spread of ripening dates. If this isn't quite enough then some of the late ripening eaters can always be picked early and cooked. I see little point in growing cider apples unless you are a particularly avid cider maker/drinker. Perfectly acceptable cider can be made from whatever other apples are available (see 'In The Kitchen').

This may sound like a huge number of trees and, by inference, a huge proportion of the available garden committed to this one crop. This could be the case, but there are a number of ways of minimising the space requirements. For many to think in terms of a specific fruit garden may be a mistake. Apples are actually ornamental trees, particularly when in blossom in May. If designing a new garden for the family I would include at least a couple of apples trees as an integral part of the ornamental/recreational garden. Most importantly though, it is the ability to control the size of the apple tree that makes it so useful in the domestic garden or even the allotment. Apples are rarely grown on their own roots. Instead they are grafted onto other rootstocks to reduce the vigour of the tree. Each cultivar (fruiting variety) is available on up to half a dozen different rootstocks to provide trees of different sizes.

For the small garden the rootstock M27 is probably ideal as it will only produce a tree which reaches around 1.5 metres after 10 years, when grown as a free-standing tree. Because the rootstock lacks vigour, the soil will need to be well prepared and a little more feeding and watering may be needed, but it will offer apple production in a reasonably small space. It's also good to know that trees on dwarfing rootstocks start fruiting at a much younger age than their more vigorous relatives. In this case the first apples should be available 2-3 years after planting.

Another solution to the space problem is to grow the trees in a restricted form, either as a cordon or as an espalier. In both these systems fruit trees are grown flat against a supporting structure of wires, often on a wall or fence. Such systems are clearly more work to set up than conventional free standing trees and they need considerably more pruning in their early years, but they do offer highly productive methods of producing top fruit like apples in very restricted spaces. For our purposes of fitting in a range of apple varieties in a restricted space a cordon, which allows the planting of the trees at just 0.75 metres spacing, is a good option. Thus our selection of half a dozen trees could be fitted onto as little as 5 metres of wall or fence. The cordon is also simpler to prune that the espalier form. When selecting trees for the cordon it's advisable to use a slightly more vigorous rootstock than for a free-standing tree, since the angle of growth, tight planting regime and pruning will all restrict growth. The M26 rootstock is probably the best on most soils, but if soils are poor the more vigorous MM106 would be a better choice. As a general point, whatever form of growing is chosen, if the conditions are less than ideal (e.g. thin soil, water logging, etc) always go for a more vigorous rootstock than you might otherwise have chosen.

If space is less of a problem I would still suggest growing apples on the M26 (or M106 on poor soils), but as small, conventional trees. These should grow no higher than around 3.5-4 metres with a similar spread after 10 years. Planting distances need to be broadly equal to the tree's spread, or slightly greater. The choice of the cultivar will have some influence on final tree size so it's difficult to be too specific. Planting a mini-orchard with this form of apples has a number of advantages; the trees are relatively small, making harvesting and pruning easy, and they fruit relatively young, typically 3-4 years from planting. Working on this principal I've created a small orchard of 8 apple trees and 2 pear trees in a space around 20 x 10 metres.

One of the reasons for selecting a number of apple varieties, other than continuity of supply, is to ensure pollination. No apple varieties are truly self-fertile and even those claiming to be will fruit much better in the presence of another apple tree as a pollinator. A few varieties are unable to act as pollinators, but still need a pollinator themselves. These are known as triploids since if one of these is planted you will need a total of three trees to provide mutual pollination. The situation is further complicated by the fact that not all apple trees flower at exactly the same time, but clearly for one tree to pollinate another flowering must coincide. Conventionally, cultivars are grouped into one of eight pollination groups with Group One being the earliest. There is some overlap between the groups so that a Group Two cultivar will usually pollinate Groups One and Three, but not Group Four. The simplest thing to do when choosing apple varieties to grow is to select half a dozen or so trees from two consecutive pollination groups. If this is done from the most common groups, say groups 3 and 4, the choice is not restricted too much, and we can be sure of good pollination every year. Of course, if your next door neighbour is also an apple grower the bees are no observers of property boundaries and even more options become available!

One final factor to consider when selecting apple varieties, apart from personal preferences of flavour, is disease resistance. This is not just an issue for organic growers but for all time-pressed gardeners. If we can cut out the traditional task of spraying trees by selecting those least susceptible to disease, we have a much better chance of success. Similarly, we should observe that some varieties are prone to diseases like canker when grown on poor soils. If we know that our feeding regime is likely to be a bit hit and miss due to the demands of a busy life, pick another variety which is more disease resistant. A good mail order catalogue will cover the 'cons' as well as the 'pros' of each available variety.

I'm fortunate living in Somerset, one of this country's prime apple growing areas, but if you live in less favourable areas look out for varieties described as hardy. The limiting factor is not the hardiness of the tree itself, but the susceptibility of the blossom and fruitlets to late frosts. Late flowering varieties can be particularly useful where frosts in May are common. Unless conditions are particularly severe and other more tender fruit are out of the question, decisions need to be based on growing apples under ordinary garden conditions and keeping any particularly favoured spots for more delicate fruit.

When it comes to the care and maintenance of apple trees it's important to realise that, in simple terms, winter pruning stimulates further growth of the tree, whereas summer pruning is more likely to encourage the production of fruiting buds. Thus, once the basic shape of the tree is established, the majority of the pruning should be done in late summer. To prune extensively in winter only serves to create more pruning for the following year. Summer pruning also gives the opportunity to remove any new growth badly affected by aphids or other pests before it becomes a serious problem.

The only other tasks I do to look after my apple trees are feeding with manure and wood ashes in the winter or spring and keeping the grass and weeds clear from the base of the trees in summer. The use of mulches helps greatly with this second task.

Pears

Pears are a rather more demanding crop than apples. Most of our modern varieties were developed in slightly warmer climates than ours (note the French names) and so we have a much better chance of success with pears if we are able to provide what shelter and extra warmth we can. They also require good, rich soils although, interestingly, they can cope well with excess water, but don't like an overly dry soil.

Apart from the extra need for warmth, growing pears is much like growing apples. The desire to provide that extra bit of warmth inclines many of us to attempt to grow pears against a warm wall in a restricted form (i.e. a cordon or espalier). A good crop of pears on an otherwise less than ideal site probably justifies the extra time spent on this plan. One point to remember is that the base of a warm wall is very likely to be a very dry spot, which pears will not easily tolerate. Plans need to include watering and mulches if you are to succeed.

One of the challenges with pears is the fact that although growing a tree is very easy, producing reliable crops is rather harder. Pears flower around 2 weeks earlier than the earliest apples and there are no late flowering varieties. Anything harsher than the lightest of frost when the tree is in flower is likely to kill off the blossom and put an end to that season's hopes of a harvest. Also, in poor springs the insects may not be around in sufficient numbers to do a good job of pollination. Protection and hand pollination are possible, but require considerable time, so we often end up accepting an intermittent crop.

The selection of pear varieties is governed by the same principles as with apples, but is simpler as there are fewer varieties to choose from and only a couple of choices of rootstocks. Grown on their own roots pears form large trees (20 metres high) and will take 10-20 years to start fruiting, so there is no option of going for a dwarfing rootstock. Quince A and Quince C are the usual rootstocks available, with Quince A being the more vigorous. Although slightly slower to fruit, Quince A is probably the better choice for most situations as its extra vigour copes better with imperfect soil conditions. As for variety, there are three criteria to look for; hardiness, disease resistance and flavour, of course! Although, in theory, the varieties labelled as hardy will do well in the North while the others will crop reliably in the South, I prefer to play safe and have chosen hardy varieties for my garden in Somerset.

Also, as with apples, at least a complementing pair of pear trees should be planted to provide mutual pollination. If possible I would again go for two varieties which flower together but whose fruit ripens at different times to provide a continuity of supply. Many pears have been developed to ripen in storage rather than on the tree. If growing two trees it would probably make sense to choose one of these varieties and one which ripens earlier on the tree, if storage space is available.

Plums and Related Fruits

This section covers a wide range of closely related members of the prunus family, from old fashioned gages through well-known and more modern plum varieties to the hardier damsons, bullaces and cherry plums. With such a large group generalisation can be difficult, but there are some key themes worth discussing. With such a wide family it should be possible for all but the most climatically disadvantaged UK grower to produce some fruit in most seasons without too much effort.

As a group the plum family favours rich soils with good depth and humus content. They will often tolerate heavy clay soils and the hardiest members will even cope with some water-logging. It is therefore only thin, poor soils that will need some enhancement.

The single greatest cause of failure in growing plums stems from the trees' habit of flowering very early in the spring. A false spring where the weather warms up for a few weeks and then reverts to hard frosts for a period can induce the trees to flower and then kill the blossom completely. To minimise these effects frost pockets must be avoided when planting plums. It might be better to risk later flowering apples in these places. Also, where late frosts are common it's wise to pick later flowering varieties. The variation in flowering time isn't as great as it is for apples, but a week or two's delay in flowering can sometimes mean the difference between a good crop and hardly any fruit. Growing in restricted forms against walls etc. can also help protect the more sensitive varieties, but given that these locations are in high demand I would try to select plum varieties that I can grow in the open. My trees are grown as simple bushes on the dwarfing rootstock St Julian A.

Some care is also needed in the selection of varieties as some are self-fertile and others need a pollinator. As with other tree fruit I suggest a pair or group of trees which flower together and pollinate each other, but which ripen over a period to give a succession of supply. If you only have room for one tree then clearly it must be self-fertile. It is probably for this reason that the Victoria plum is grown so widely both domestically and commercially. Victoria is self-fertile and flowering in mid season it will usually pollinate both early and late flowering varieties. It is also a more reliable cropper than most varieties. Unfortunately, many people feel that its flavour is a little bland, preferring some of the less reliable and lighter cropping gages – c'est la vie!

The only real pest problem I've had when growing plums and their relatives is the plum moth. This lays its eggs on embryonic fruit and we end up with small pink grubs in the fruit. The traditional insecticide remedy is not an option for the organic grower so I tend to live with the problem, keeping it under control by cleaning up and destroying all infected fruit to prevent the next generation of the moth surviving. This pest also tends to cause premature ripening of the fruit, so if the first small batch of fruit to ripen is removed, checked and destroyed if infected, the remainder is usually found to be clear. Working this way the percentage lost to this pest is small.

Some of the less well-known plum relatives are also worthy of consideration as they need little looking after and frequently remain productive under harsh conditions. For example, I know of an old damson tree on a smallholding in Snowdonia which fruits heavily, despite being at around 500 metres above sea level and being rooted in almost permanently water-logged soil. Damsons, bullaces and cherry plums are genetically close to the wild ancestors of the domesticated plum. All produce small, dense trees (although the cherry plum can get quite big if not cut back) which can be used in a boundary hedge and to provide wind breaks around more sensitive crops. In such circumstances they will still crop satisfactorily and give a useful source of fruit for cooking for no more effort than the trouble of picking. In all an ideal crop for the busy gardener, and growing fruit in the hedge gains an extra crop from land which is otherwise unproductive.

Cherries

I have to start by confessing that cherries are not a fruit with which I've had much success to date, but I intend to persevere. Not only do I particularly like cherries, but they are also ready earlier in the year than most other top fruit and are therefore particularly welcome.

The biggest difficulty with this fruit is not getting the tree to produce, but getting hold of the fruit before the birds do. Our common garden birds are quite happy to take cherries before they are properly ripe and so gain an unfair advantage over the grower when it comes to harvesting. Clearly the trees have to be netted to retain a crop through to harvest, but this isn't quite as simple as it sounds. Netting a free-standing, fully grown cherry tree at a height above 10 metres is no joke!

There are two realistic ways of producing cherries in this manner and both require planning from the outset. The first is to grow the tree in a restricted form (usually a fan) against a wall, so that the netting can be attached with relative ease to the top of the wall and anchored in the ground. This is a great deal easier that attempting to net even a fairly small tree grown as a standard. If a wall isn't available, then even a free standing, fan-trained tree grown on wires between stout posts will be easier to net than a standard tree.

The second solution is to grow the tree on an extremely dwarfing rootstock (Giselle 5) and grow it within a fruit cage. This type of rootstock has only recently become available to the domestic grower and as such is still a little untried, but if the producers claims are correct it should, with some training, produce a fruiting tree that never gets above 2 metres in height. In view of the likely demands on space within a fruit cage I would suggest that training it into a fan shape is probably also a good idea, but it is not strictly necessary from the point of view of growing the cherries.

Until recently cherries were only available on Malling F12/1 rootstock, which produces huge, totally impractical trees and on Colt rootstocks which are best described as moderately dwarfing. Colt is fine to produce a tree to cover a wall 4 metres long and 2.5 metres high, but in many circumstances it can still be too vigorous for the home farmer. I have high hopes of the new Giselle 5 rootstock as it should produce a genuine dwarf tree. Mine is only 3 years old and was badly damaged by deer on my allotment last year. It is now recovering, but it has suffered a severe setback, and I'm still not sure of its eventual size and productivity.

Having mentioned fan trained trees several times in this section I feel that it is only fair to point out that this is probably one of the more difficult forms in which to train trees. A good book on the details of training fruit trees is a necessity (see Further Reading). The tasks of pruning twice a year and tying in branches is not particularly time consuming, but it may well be one step too far for the busy gardener. To simplify matters it is probably worth considering buying trees that have already been trained to the basic fan structure. These cost a bit more than the maiden tree, but if the pruning task is reduced to one of maintaining the existing structure rather than creating a new one, there is much less to go wrong.

Nice warm garden or house walls to grow our fruit against are always at a premium and I have already suggested that the best site should be reserved for pear trees or even peaches. It's therefore worth knowing that if the only wall available is a cold, north facing one, morrello cherries (a sharp tasting fruit grown to be cooked) will crop very happily there. The sweeter dessert cherries need more light and warmth, but at least this is one very useful crop which will thrive in this unlikely spot and can be netted against the birds as suggested above.

Growing Nuts

Nut growing is still an experiment for me. However, I am convinced that it is possible for the amateur grower to produce significant quantities of a range of nuts with a minimum of effort. I'm currently growing hazels, an almond and a walnut. I would like to fit in a sweet chestnut too, as they can be very productive, but I need to work out how it can be done given the limited space available and the potential size of the tree.

This issue of space is significant, particularly with species that require more than one tree to be grown for pollination purposes, but I think I've got round the issue in the case of the hazels (cobnuts/filberts) by growing wild hazels in my boundary hedge as pollinators. With regard to the other species, the good news is that nurseries are constantly coming up with new compact varieties, many of which claim to be self-fertile. I chose Broadview as my walnut and Robijn as my almond. As when choosing fruit trees, I also picked varieties claiming good disease resistance. Both trees have established themselves, but have not yet come into production.

The only obvious pest limiting nut production is the grey squirrel, which is common now to most UK woodlands and gardens. They are said to not like crossing wide open spaces without tree cover, but few of us have the luxury of enough space to take advantage of this fact. My solution at the moment lies with my Jack Russell terrier, Sally, who is obsessed with chasing squirrels, but we shall have to see how effective she is when faced with a determined raid on the nut trees.

Chapter Nine
In The Kitchen

It may be reasonable to assume that because the gardener has made the effort to produce a particular vegetable, he or she has a clear idea of what to do with it. In most cases I'm sure this is the case, but it may be that some of the ideas contained in this book have encouraged the growing of something new, hence it seems appropriate to add a few ideas on what can be done with the produce. I've also included a few suggestions that could be lumped under the heading of 'What to do when I grew more than I meant to'. Some items are full blown recipes, others are simply ideas specific to the crops grown.

I very rarely bother measuring the minor ingredients in a dish, so I've given an indication of what I do rather than the precise weights and measures. The major ingredients are weighed to let you know the scale I'm working on.

West Country Onion Soup
(4 generous servings)

This recipe is included because, apart from it being very tasty, it provides a suggestion of what do to with an excess of onions. I'm writing this in the middle of a particularly wet summer, during which I was a little late in getting in my over-wintered onions. Some are showing signs of damage and clearly won't store for long, so another recipe to use them in bulk was called for. This is my own variation on the French classic, but substituting local ingredients and making some minor changes to the procedure for the sake of convenience. I make my own cider so this dish really is home produced.

1 generous lump of butter (about 30-40g)
1 good splash of olive oil (about 20ml)
About 750g sliced onions (weighed after all waste has been removed)

2 cloves of garlic, chopped
1 litre stock (home made or from cubes)
350ml dry cider
A big pinch of granulated sugar (about 10g)
4 slices from a small, rounded loaf of bread
Enough sliced mature cheddar to cover the bread
A dash of Worcestershire sauce
Salt and pepper to taste.

Melt the butter with the oil in a large pan and add the onions, garlic and sugar. Cook gently, stirring from time to time. After about half an hour, if the mixture hasn't started to brown, turn the heat up and stir continuously until it does. Don't worry about a few brown bits sticking to the bottom of the pan, these will come off when the liquid is added and will help to colour the soup.

When you are satisfied with the colour add the stock and the cider, cover with a lid, bring the mixture up to the boil and simmer gently for about an hour. Before serving, add the Worcestershire sauce and salt and pepper to taste.

While the soup is cooking the bread needs to be thoroughly dried out. The easiest way to do this is to bake it for about 20 minutes on a baking tray in a medium oven, although it can be achieved in a toaster. When you are ready to serve, put the bread (now large croutons) on the grill pan, cover them with the cheese and put them under a hot grill until the cheese is bubbling. Serve the soup into bowls and carefully drop a cheese covered crouton onto the surface of each.

Pissaladière
(Serves 4)

This is another recipe I've used when I have a lot of onions that won't keep. It appears the French are particularly adept at the bulk consumption of onions! The recipe is basically a variation on a pizza using caramelised onions as the main topping. I always prefer to make my own pizza style bases, but there is no reason why this topping shouldn't be served on bought pizza bases.

For the onion mixture:
2 kg onions, trimmed and roughly sliced
1 generous lump of butter (about 30-40g)
2-3 good splashes of olive oil (about 50ml)
2 cloves of garlic, chopped / 2-3 Bay leaves
A big pinch granulated sugar (about 10g)
A wineglass of white wine or cider
About 30g finely grated hard cheese – pecorino, parmesan or firm cheddar
A good handful of finely chopped herbs – thyme, oregano or marjoram

Additional, optional toppings:
Olives, black or green – probably about a dozen
Capers – rather more (pickled nasturtium seeds make a good substitute)
Anchovy fillets – a small tin/jar 50g

For the base:
350g bread flour (can be white, wholemeal or a mixture of the two)
1 good splash of olive oil
1 small pinch of salt / 1 generous pinch of granulated sugar
1 sachet of quick acting yeast
200ml warm water.

Start as in the previous recipe by gently cooking the onions, garlic, bay leaves and sugar in the oil and melted butter, stirring occasionally. Once the mixture has softened and started to reduce in volume the heat can be gradually increased, and with it the frequency of the stirring. The idea is to caramelise the onions without burning too much of the mixture into the bottom of the pan. With this large quantity of onions it will probably take about an hour's cooking and will result in a 75% reduction in volume. When the mixture is a nice brown colour remove the bay leaves, add the wine and mix it round for a moment to dislodge any bits suck to the pan. Then put on one side until the base is ready.

The base I use is just a standard bread base I would normally use for a pizza. Other cooks will have their own versions. I simply add the dry ingredients plus the oil to the flour and mix them together. To create a quantity of warm water for bread making I mix one third of the quantity of boiling water with two thirds of water from the cold tap. I then tip most of this water into the flour mixture and mix it to make a dough. The reason a little water is held back is that the water required is always a bit variable: sometimes a little more is needed, sometimes a little less. Once a workable dough has been created it should be kneaded on a floured surface for a few minutes until it's smooth and elastic. It's then smeared with a little more olive oil and left in a covered bowl in a warm place to rise. It should take about half an hour to double in size, at which point it can be kneaded again and rolled out to fit a standard baking tray. The tray should be greased before the dough is fitted and then it can all be left in a warm place for a further half hour to rise for a second time.

To complete the dish, spread the onion mixture on the surface of the bread dough and sprinkle first with the grated cheese and then with the finely chopped herbs. The pissaladière can now be baked like this or extra toppings can be added first. A scattering of olives or capers makes a tasty addition, or a lattice pattern of anchovy fillets looks attractive. Whether or not any extras are added, the pissaladière should be baked at 200°C for 20 minutes. It can be served either hot or cold.

Blackberry Sponge
(Serves about 5)

This is a quick and easy way of making a hot winter pudding from the bags of frozen blackberries in the freezer and it's something that the kids will actually choose to eat! I try to start the winter season with at least a couple of 1kg bags of frozen blackberries gathered during autumn walks in the local fields and orchards and this is the principal way in which they are used over the months ahead. When picking wild blackberries I would recommend only gathering them well away from roads and only from field boundaries that are unlikely to have been sprayed. Soft fruit is best frozen by spreading it out in a thin layer on a tray in the freezer and then bagging it up when solid. If frozen in a bag to start with, a solid, unusable block will result. Working this way the berries are loose and easy to use.

300g frozen – or fresh blackberries
125g self-raising flour
125g margarine
125g sugar
2 eggs
1 tsp baking powder
1 dsp extra sugar

Pour the blackberries into a casserole dish, throw in the extra spoon of sugar and mix briefly. Put it to one side somewhere warm while the berries (if frozen) defrost. In the meantime put all the other ingredients in a bowl and mix them together to make an even cake mixture. If the mixture is very thick and difficult to mix it may be necessary to add a few drops of water (but literally only a few drops!). Once the blackberries have defrosted, spoon the cake mixture over them and put the dish into the oven pre-heated to 150°C. It should take around 45 minutes, or a little longer if the blackberries were very cold when put in. Either way the sponge will need checking towards the end to make sure its cooked right through.

My family like me to serve the sponge hot, with cream.

Self-Sufficient Winter Fry-Up
(serves 4 but may need enlarging after a hard afternoon's digging)

This is a dish devised to work almost entirely on what I've got in the garden in late winter. I have to admit that the bacon isn't home produced, but all the vegetable ingredients are usually either in the ground or in store in late January or February and by then our hens should have started laying again, after their dark season break.

450g Jerusalem artichokes
450g potatoes
250g sliced bacon – smoked for preference
1 large onion
2-3 cloves of garlic
1 good bunch of kale – variable depending on how much you like it!
4 large eggs – home produced if possible.
Oil to fry in
Salt and pepper to season.
Squeeze of lemon juice or drop of vinegar

The worst part of this dish is preparing the artichokes. These need to be peeled and chopped into discs about 0.5cm thick. Artichokes tend to discolour if any cut surfaces are left open to the air and, although this isn't really important, the discolouration does spoil the colour of the dish. I drop the cut pieces into a large pan of cold water acidified with a little lemon juice or vinegar as I'm working. The potatoes are also peeled and chopped into similar sized chunks and thrown into the same water. Then prepare the kale, removing the thickest stems and any damaged bits. Wash and place it in a steaming tray to fit over the top of the large pan containing the artichokes and potatoes, both still in the slightly acidic water. Bring to the boil and simmer for about 5 minutes until the artichokes and potatoes are just softening. Put the kale on one side and strain the other vegetables.

While the artichokes and potatoes are cooking, chop the onion into rough slices and the garlic more finely. Remove the rind from the bacon and cut it up into small slices. Fry the onion gently until it is soft and vaguely transparent.

Take a large pan, add whatever oil you are using to fry in and bring it up to a moderate heat. Tip in the now relatively dry potato and artichoke mixture. Fry this, turning it occasionally as it starts to brown and add the cooked onion and the raw garlic. While this mix is cooking, return to the frying pan and cook the bacon slices. When the vegetable mixture has started to brown add the now cooked bacon and the lightly steamed kale, season with salt and pepper and stir to combine. While the completed mixture is receiving a final few minutes cooking as a whole, add more oil to the frying pan and prepare to fry the eggs. The mixture from the main pan can be served out onto 4 plates and kept warm under the grill while the eggs are fried and one placed on top of each steaming pile of vegetables and bacon. A little freshly ground black pepper sprinkled over the top of the eggs is all that's needed to complete a delicious, home produced winter supper.

Courgettes and Garlic

Courgette recipes are always useful as it's so easy to end up with a glut of this vegetable. To serve as a vegetable accompaniment to a meat dish I simply fry a pan full of sliced courgettes in olive oil with 3-4 cloves of garlic. I don't usually bother with trying to use salt to remove some of the moisture from the courgettes before cooking. The courgettes are simply fried gently in an open pan. Chopped garlic is dropped on top to be incorporated as the courgettes are turned over to brown on both sides. It normally takes 20-30 minutes to cook a pan full, depending on how full the pan actually is and what shade (golden brown through to almost black) is preferred.

Cockerel in Cider

If you become a chicken keeper and start breeding your own birds you will inevitably end up with surplus cockerels. The males of some breeds of poultry are easily identifiable at hatching or shortly after and so can be dispatched. However, with many crosses and hybrid birds it can be very difficult to separate male from female until they start to exhibit adult behaviour and plumage. At this point, typically around 3-4 months, the surplus males must be removed. Having gone to the trouble and expense of raising them thus far I regard them as a good meal and therefore include a typical recipe I use.

These days we are used to buying poultry that has been bred for meat and is young and very tender. Our home raised birds are better, regarded more as a by-product of our egg production and as such, although they may well be a little scrawnier and tougher, they are always more flavoursome. As such, if we treat them the same as a roasting chicken bought from the butcher, we are likely to end up with a rather tough, dry roast. A longer, slower stew/casserole approach works much better. Here is an example based on the type of ingredients I have to hand in the garden and store cupboard. It is based on a single bird of the typical size I find myself with, and makes a meal for 2.

1 cockerel, around 750g when plucked, drawn and jointed
400ml home made cider
1 large onion
2 carrots, about 200g, peeled and chopped
2 cloves garlic
A bunch of fresh herbs as available
A little oil for frying
Salt and pepper for seasoning

If you can be bothered to joint the bird completely it makes the cooking and eating processes a bit easier, but I often just cut it in half. After preparing the meat, brown the surfaces, particularly the skin side, with a little oil in a hot pan. Shake or stir the pieces around so that all the sides become nicely browned. It's worth spending the time to do this well as I find the skin rather rubbery if it is not well browned before stewing.

Next, transfer the meat to a casserole dish/ metal pot with a lid – the kind that can be used both on the top of the stove and in the oven. Add all the other ingredients. The quantity of cider can be a bit variable depending on the size of the pot. The idea is to have enough liquid to just cover the meat. If there isn't enough cider, a little water can be added.

Now bring the pot up to a gentle boil on the top of the stove and, once boiling, transfer into a moderate oven (160°C) for about an hour. Cooking times will vary a bit as some birds will be more tender than others, so it's a good idea to check at around that time and give it a little longer if necessary. I regard it as done when the meat is starting to come away from the bones.

Home Made Ice Cream

In my view this is one of the best ways of using surplus soft fruit. It is also a way in which part of a glut of fruit can be preserved and wheeled out later in the year, but not as a dull, preserved fruit concoction, but rather as a delicious treat. To be worthy of inclusion in the busy cook's repertoire it does require the purchase of an ice cream maker, but the small versions of these are not terribly expensive and the results are both delicious and very easily achieved. Quantities will vary with the size of your ice cream maker. Mine claims to have a 1.5 litre capacity and recommends the following combination:

500g strawberries
300ml double cream
100g caster sugar

The procedure is to crush, coarsely mash or briefly process the fruit. Separately mix the sugar into the cream and then combine the crushed fruit with the sweetened cream in the ice cream maker. Leave it to churn until the correct consistency is achieved. This takes about half an hour.

I've found a very successful blackcurrant ice cream variation by reducing the fruit content to about 300g (because of the sharp flavour) and giving the blackcurrants a very short cook first; just enough to start to break the berries up. After this the fruit has to be allowed to cool before adding it to the ice cream maker.

Drinking The Crop

For centuries people have produced their alcoholic beverages at home from a combination of home grown and bought in ingredients. In the days before the availability of imported tea and coffee these were a vital part of the typical Briton's diet and lifestyle. We must ask ourselves how we can continue this practice in the modern world using as much of our own produce as possible, thus giving ourselves food security and minimising food miles, but also working in a way that makes efficient use of our time?

It is perfectly possible and completely legal to make highly drinkable wines, beers and ciders at home, for personal consumption. The challenge comes in making them from predominately home produced ingredients. Many people in Britain make 'country wines' at home from garden produce. However, in most cases the production is highly dependant on large quantities of bought in sugar. A typical 5 litre batch of wine will need at least 1kg of sugar to provide the expected alcohol concentration of around 12% by volume. Grape juice, when produced in a warm climate, already contains these sugar levels, but most fruit, vegetables and flowers available to the home wine maker contain nothing like enough. The sugar must therefore be added from another commercial source. Whilst this is a perfectly effective technique it is moving away from being a home grown product and starts to raise the issue of quality of supply. Organically produced cane sugar is readily available but it will have been transported thousands of miles to get here: beet sugar is usually a British product but I've rarely seen an organic brand on sale. Either way, to use it in large quantities would destroy the satisfaction of producing a beverage from the garden. Alternatively, if you organise your growing to achieve a good supply of home grown grapes, added sugar should be unnecessary and wine from the garden will become a realistic objective.

Producing home made beer is also a popular hobby in the UK. However, this is also highly reliant on bought in ingredients. The main constituent of beer is malted barley which, although technically possible to produce at home (i.e. grow the grain and then germinate it, roast it and extract the malt), requires a very lengthy and time consuming process. Having tried once to produce beer by malting my own grain I would not recommend it; it was great fun as an experiment but it was a lot of work to produce a fairly poor product. Hops, the other main ingredient in beer, are easily produced at home, but as only around 50-100g of the dried flowers are needed to flavour 10 litres of beer, compared to around 3 kg of malted grain, it's stretching things a little to regard the product as home grown on account of the hops alone. However, this can be an interesting diversion if the time is available and at least good quality malt grains are UK produced. If hops are to be grown it is probably wise to source a modern, so called dwarf variety (plants are available from a number of the major mail order nurseries) as these are much more manageable in the garden, only growing to about 3 metres.

In my view cider is the ideal home produced drink. At its simplest it is nothing more than fermented apple juice. It has a number of very positive attributes from the perspective of the home grower; it can be produced from any type or combination of types of apples, it doesn't need a lot of extra bought in ingredients, apples are easy to grow or obtain in fairly large quantities and the cider itself is quite easy to produce. Since apples are the fruit best adapted to grow in the British climate it makes a great deal of sense to make maximum use of them in this way, rather than struggling to produce a good crop of grapes, which will always be more marginal in the UK.

Apple trees are frequently one of the first things that anyone interested in producing their own food looks to plant in a new garden and a number of trees are planted to give variety and continuity of supply. As the trees start to mature their productivity increases exponentially and so it is not uncommon to find, say 8-10 years after planting, that the supply of apples exceeds the demand and new uses have to be found. It also means that surplus apples may frequently be available from friends or neighbours for little more than the trouble of collection. I would want to be sure that the trees hadn't been subjected to chemical sprays before using such free produce, but people whose trees massively over supply their requirements are not particularly likely to be avid sprayers – why bother?

Cider production tends to use rather a large quantity of apples. I usually use wine makers' fermentation jars, also known as demijohns, to brew my cider which, being fairly old, hold an imperial gallon (around 4.5 litres) each. As a basis for measurement these can lead to some slightly irregular figures. However, to fill such a jar the juice from around 7-9kg of apples is required. In an ideal world I would use traditional cider apples for all my brews. These apples have been selected over the centuries to produce a juice with the right combination of sugars, acids and tannins which, when fermented and matured, will give a balanced, refreshing cider. Since this is not usually a practical proposition I will use whatever combination of apples I can get hold of and then adjust the flavour of the juice slightly as necessary. The juice of a predominately eating apple mix will tend to taste bland, lacking a sharp edge. I therefore add the juice of a lemon and a mug of strong (black!) tea to each 4.5 litre brew to boost the acid and tannin levels. If cooking apples have been used it may be that the acidity is fine, but further tannin is still needed.

Traditional cider makers never add further sugar to the apple juice prior to fermentation. Providing the apples were fully ripe on pressing, the juice should contain enough sugar to provide a reasonable alcohol level (say 5-7% by volume). It's quite important to ensure a reasonable level of alcohol, not only for the effects when consumed, but also the alcohol ensures that the cider will keep. The only way of confirming the initial sugar levels in the juice is by using a wine-makers' hydrometer. This is a simple device that floats in a sample of the juice and measures its specific gravity (the density of the liquid relative to the density of water). This works on the simple understanding that the more sugar a liquid contains, the higher its specific gravity will be. If the specific gravity of the apple juice is found too low a small amount of extra sugar can be added. Details of the calculations will usually be provided with the hydrometer, but in my experience 100-150g in the 4.5 litre brew has always been sufficient. However, many home cider makers don't worry about such a scientific approach and simply make sure that the mix of apples for juicing includes as proportion of ripe eating apples to boost the overall sugar levels.

To produce my cider I start by washing the apples in the kitchen sink, just to remove any mud, grass and leaves etc. I also remove any obviously bad ones, although I don't worry about minor bruises or bird pecks etc. I don't fiddle at this stage, an apple is either in or out. The apples are then cut in half, or quarters if particularly large, and crushed in a large saucepan with a heavy piece of wood. This is done in small batches leaning over the saucepan placed on the floor. The piece of wood is an old oak table leg roughly 1metre x 10cm x 10cm. There is no need to core the apples before doing this. It is possible to obtain apple crushers designed specifically for the purpose, but I've never wanted to spend the money. The next stage is to press the apple pulp to obtain the juice. I have, in the past, experimented with improvised apple presses, but have found the ones I made were just too slow. I therefore bought a purpose made small fruit press which will take my 8kg or so of apple pulp in two loads.

Once I have a demijohn full of apple juice and have made any adjustments for tannins and acidity, I add a specialist wine yeast. It is probable that the apple juice would ferment of its own accord, but having gone to all the trouble of producing the juice I don't want to risk it. The demijohn can then be sealed with a fermentation lock and left at room temperature to for the juice to ferment. Cider is a very well-behaved brew compared to beer or some wines: it ferments gently without foaming up and will pop away in the corner of the kitchen for a few months. Don't worry that your newly pressed apple juice has an unpleasant brownish colour, rather than the golden yellow of the highly purified version from the supermarket. As the fermentation draws to a close much of the material clouding the cider will drop to the bottom of the jar and can be left behind when the cider is bottled.

Within a couple of months bubbles should have stopped popping through the fermentation lock and the brew should look considerably clearer, although the colour will vary from pale yellow to a golden brown colour, depending on the apples used. At this stage it will taste very dry and probably rather rough and disappointing. The clear cider must now be racked off the deposit at the bottom of the demijohn and matured for a period. This is done with a plastic siphon tube which sucks the clear cider out of the jar without disturbing the yeasty debris on the bottom. As I always want to reduce the number of operations to a minimum, I usually bottle it at this point, although many people would opt for maturing it in a clean jar for some months before bottling. I also prefer cider to be slightly sparkling and so, when bottling, I cheat and add half a teaspoon of sugar to each bottle (I re-use old 500ml beer bottles). The sugar goes in before the cider via a funnel, otherwise it tends to spill over the outside of the bottle. The bottles are then sealed with metal bottle tops using a capping tool and tapped into place with a wooden mallet.

One of the most important things to remember in producing cider is to leave it to mature. Traditionally, I'm told, the cider made each autumn was to 'help with the hay-making' next summer and it wasn't to be touched until then. In some parts of the country there was a tradition of sampling the new season's cider when the first cuckoo of summer was heard. This November to May/June maturation is a good guideline, but it will often continue to improve for at least a year. One other slightly less rustic point to make is that, although we may have images of cider presses and open vats in barns with animals all around, hygiene is really important. Make sure that all equipment, presses, bottles, demijohns etc. are scrupulously clean before use.

Chapter Ten
Record Keeping

Although the idea of spending valuable time creating records may sound like the delusions of an over zealous bureaucrat, I find my records invaluable. This source of vital information saves me considerable time rather that wastes it. I also find that I can use time for recording my activities which isn't available for gardening. My own record system in the form of a simple A5 size diary sits in my desk draw at work. I find 10 minutes scribbling each Monday lunchtime is enough to record my weekend activities.

Records serve a number of purposes. Firstly, they force me to be honest about whether a certain crop really is worth the trouble in terms of the time and expense required to produce it. If my records show that last year my Brussels sprout crop only produced enough for a couple of meals, am I going to go to the trouble of raising seedlings, planting them out, watering in dry spells, protecting from pests etc, this year? If I am, I will need to think seriously about what went wrong last time and try to do something different this year. My records should give me enough information, particularly when things went badly, to come up with a different approach such as changing the variety, or simply growing something completely different.

Records enable better decision making when it comes to questions such as "If I want to plant out some good sized courgette plants as soon as possible after the last frost, when should I sow the seed in the pots on the windowsill?" Rather than relying on the rather vague information available in gardening books or on the backs of seed packets, a simple check on what I did last year and how well it worked will provide the best possible guidance. Obviously, spring weather conditions are never exactly the same two years on the trot, but at least the information is specific to my own plot and the variety grown. If I've remembered to record date sown, date potted on, date started hardening off and date planted out, together with any important comments (e.g. Damn!! Too early - killed by frost, or got a bit pot bound while waiting for better weather), it should be a simple matter to adjust the sowing date this year. It's worth pointing out that the sowing date is the only date in the lifecycle of the productive plant over which the grower has complete control. All others can be varied, but the plant will be doing its own thing and may suffer as a result, so it's worth getting this date right.

Most of us set out to produce as much good food as our time and land will permit. These records show the success we are having (or not as the case may be!). Sometimes, particularly with crops that are harvested a bit at a time, its easy to forget just how much we've produced and what an effect it's having on our household economy. Checking the record and seeing the quantities produced and the year on year increase as more land is brought into optimal usage is very satisfying and helps to motivate me when life seems too busy. One particular point I like to record each year is the date on which last year's home grown potatoes run out. It's been a great source of satisfaction over the years to see it creep later, from late autumn to New Year and now on into early spring.

The preceding discussion gives a good indication of what to record, but in summary it simply needs to be enough to enable you to work out what you did when and where and what the results were. Usually I only record sowing, planting out and harvesting, but try to record quantities and varieties throughout, with the odd comment where significant. I always intend to weigh everything and record precise details, but usually fail, particularly when it comes to the odd leek pulled in a hurry or a handful of strawberries picked and eaten quickly. As a result quite a bit of my diary weights and measures are estimates rather than absolute facts, but these are much better than nothing. It can be very tempting when a disaster occurs, as it does to us all from time to time, to forget about it, not recording it and moving on. This is foolish as it is highly unlikely anything will be done to prevent it happening again next year or the year after.

I tend also to make brief notes about the weather. These are not very scientific, but they provide key background information. The weekly notes may be as simple as, 'Hot and dry all week – still no rain' or 'Frosts several nights this week'. One year I noted that it didn't rain between 15th March and 7th May and I've also noted that many of my over-wintered onions have bolted. These facts are clearly related. What will I do differently next time? I haven't got time to water this crop throughout the spring, so maybe I'll try putting a mulch down next time, or I'll see if I can find a variety of onion that is more resistant to bolting.

How you choose to record your progress is up to you but I urge you to do so; it really does make the best use of your future time if referred to regularly.

In Conclusion...

There is clearly much more to taking control of our diet and producing our own food than simply deciding which crops to produce. Other than our time limitations, the biggest single factor governing how we approach our food production is the amount, condition and location of the land available to us. Very few of us are in the fortunate position of having even a modest $50m^2$ (10 x 5 metre) plot as part of the back garden on which to grow our fruit and veg, since not only are modern housing plots ridiculously small, but also food production has to compete with the other demands of a family garden. The solution for most of us is to rent an allotment, but this, even if available in the locality, usually adds further pressure on our busy lives when travel time is added in. Things are never simple!

The objective of this book is to suggest ways in which these dilemmas of modern living can be resolved. The Basic Plan, whether enhanced with more complex variations or not, was designed to be run on my allotment during a particularly busy period in my life which included 2 house moves and a job that involved quite a lot of overseas travel. It is an ideal way of producing a significant quantity of basic food without much effort, and certainly with no more than a 1 hour visit per week. I would be the last person to pretend that the produce is particularly exciting, but it is a starting point. From there it should be possible to add smaller quantities of more exciting crops, grown perhaps in a small bed, a group of pots or even a mini-greenhouse back at home where these can be tended in a few minutes most days during the summer growing season. When these two growing locations are worked in tandem, a very significant contribution to the family's vegetable requirements can be produced.

For those able to take a slightly more long term view, fruit production offers excellent value in return for the time invested. If the ground is well prepared, suitable disease resistant varieties chosen and mulches used to minimise weeding, the most onerous task with most fruit growing is also the most enjoyable one; picking the crop. True, most of the work has to be done 1-4 years (depending on the fruit concerned) before much produce is collected, which can be a challenge to our self-discipline and patience, but it is really worth investing a little time and money each year to build up the fruit collection.

Total self-sufficiency, even in terms of fruit and vegetable production, is still something to which I aspire rather than have in my immediate grasp. However, I believe the approach I've developed here has made it possible to make home grown produce a major part of my family's diet, while still leading a relatively normal life with 'normally excessive' working hours and living in a normal British home. As always, there are still improvements to the plans to be made and new techniques to try. I hope that these ideas will not only inform, but stimulate readers to experiment and devise better and more effective approaches of their own.

List of Vegetable Crops by Family

As discussed in Chapters 4 and 5, annual vegetable crops need to be rotated so that a single crop or a closely related one is not grown on the same land in successive seasons. To achieve this it is clearly necessary to know the main family groupings of the vegetables under discussion. This Annex lists the common family groups and also the 'one-offs' (i.e. where single members of a family are grown). These can be particularly useful and can be fitted in anywhere without worrying about what went before or what is to follow on.

In the table I've named each family after one of its most widely grown members, but included the Latin name for the sake of correctness and to allow cross-referencing.

The Onion Family

(Allium or Amaryllidaceae)

Chives

Garlic

Leeks

Onions

Shallots

The Bean Family

(Leguminosae)

Asparagus Pea

Broad Bean

French Bean

Pea

Runner Bean

The Lettuce Family

(Asteraceae)

Artichoke - Globe

Artichoke - Jerusalem

Cardoon

Chicory

Endive

Lettuce

Salsify

Scorzonera

The Beet Family

(Chenopodiaceae)

Beetroot

Chard

Spinache

Good King Henry

Quinoa

The Cabbage Familiy
(Brassicaceae)
Broccoli
Brussel Sprouts
Cabbages
Cauliflower
Kale
Kohlrabi
Mustard (green manure crop)
Radish
Swede
Turnip

The Tomato Family
(Solanaceae)
Aubergine
Chilli Pepper
Potato
Sweet Pepper
Tomato

The One Offs
Sweet Corn

Asparagus
New Zealand Spinach
Corn Salad

The Cucumber Family
(Cucurbitaceae)
Courgette
Cucumber
Marrow
Squash
Pumpkin
Melon

The Carrot Family
(Umbelliferea)
Carrot
Celeriac
Celery
Fennel
Parsnip

Further Reading

This book has touched on a number of themes. In exploring them further I have found the following very valuable:

The Vegetable & Herb Expert by Dr. D. G. Hessayon
published by Expert Books

This is an invaluable little handbook which provides a page or two on the details of how to grow all the common vegetable crops. It is an excellent quick reference guide when you want to check planting distances and sowing times etc. It also has very useful details of pests and diseases to enable quick identification and resolution.

The Fruit Garden Explained by Harry Baker
published by the RHS

This is a definitive work on how to grow fruit in this country. Although some things change and new varieties are developed, I find it an excellent guide on how to prune fruit trees.

The Complete Book of Self-Sufficiency by John Seymour
published by Dorling Kindersley

This has been described as the bible of self-sufficiency and is compulsive reading for anyone who wants to live truly independently.

How to Make a Forest Garden by Patrick Whitefield
published by Permanent Publications

The forest gardening technique set out lucidly by Patrick Whitefield which, if taken in its entirety, provides a fascinating alternative approach to minimum input growing. On a more selective basis I find his tips and information on fruit growing particularly useful.

Scotts of Merriot Catalogue
(Now Merriot Garden Centre)

This catalogue purports to contain brief details of all apple trees available to the home gardener in the UK, plus a wide range of other fruit trees. I find it an excellent quick reference when attempting to select fruit trees.

How to Make a Forest Garden by Patrick Whitefield
published by Permanent Publications
The forest gardening technique set out lucidly by Patrick Whitefield which, if taken in its entirety, provides a fascinating alternative approach to minimum input growing. On a more selective basis I find his tips and information on fruit growing particularly useful.

The Four Season Harvest by Elliot Coleman
published by Chelsea Green Publishing
Although aimed at the small scale commercial grower the book really opens up the possibilities for growing out of season using glasshouses and polytunnels.

The River Cottage Cookbook by Hugh Fernley-Whittingstall
published by Harper Collins
Another fascinating self-sufficiency book which contains some excellent recipes based on produce that most home growers are likely to find on their hands – I never realised you could do so many things with a courgette!

Free-Range Poultry by Katie Thear
published by Whittet Books
Although many of the examples quoted are aimed more at commercial producers than domestic, I found this a very useful book when starting to keep hens.

Best Soft Fruit by Stefan Buchatzki
published by Hamlyn
The author takes a particularly wide definition of soft fruit which I find very useful, as are his explanations of pruning techniques.

The Transition Handbook by Rob Hopkins
published by Green Books
This is an excellent read for anyone who is uncertain about the need for personal and local independence and resilience. It is also a very positive and encouraging take on a potential world crisis: the "Transition Movement is more of a party than a protest rally."

55

Resource List

The Organic Gardening Catalogue
www.organiccatalogue.com 0845 1301304

An excellent all round source of vegetable seeds, fruit trees and bushes and gardening sundries. It contains a very good range of organic and the overall selection of vegetable seeds offered is wide and good value for money. An easy to use website too!

The Real Seed Catalogue
www.realseeds.co.uk 01239 821107

A small collection of rare, heirloom and unusual non-hybrid vegetables selected with the home grower in mind, but with many interesting and useful options at reasonable prices.

Victoriana Nurseries
www.victoriananursery.co.uk 01233 740529

Victoriana Nurseries provides a range of high quality fruit and vegetable seeds and plants, specialising in the best of those grown in times past. I particularly like their tall "Victorian" peas.

Scotts Nurseries (Merriott Garden Centre Ltd.)
www.scottsnurseries.co.uk 01460 72306
A wide range of fruit trees including several hundred apple varieties all on a selection of rootstocks, with excellent stock at reasonable prices.

Garden Organic (Formerly the Henry Doubleday Research Association)Heritage Seed Programme
www.gardenorganic.org.uk 024 7630 3517

The Heritage Seed Programme is a subscription service providing members with de-listed vegetable seeds that are no longer available from commercial sources. Sometimes the quantities of seeds on offer (particularly for larger seeded varieties) may be small, but the programme provides a unique access to some valuable and historic vegetables.

Suttons Seeds
www.suttons.co.uk 0844 9220606

Deacons Nursery
www.deaconsnurseryfruits.co.uk 01983 840750
A specialist fruit nursery with a wide range of apple, cherry, plum,
pear, soft fruits, grapes and hops.

Thompson and Morgan
www.thompson-morgan.com 0844 2485383

Moreveg UK
moreveg.co.uk 01823 681302

Dobies of Devon
www.dobies.co.uk 0844 7017625

Tuckers Seeds
www.tuckers-seeds.co.uk 01364 652233

Two Wests and Elliott
www.twowests.co.uk 01246 451077

All of the above supply flower and vegetable seeds, plug plants,
fruit trees and bushes and a wide range of gardening equipment and
sundries for sale either online or by catalogue.

Fields of Food
www.fieldsoffood.co.uk
An online auction site providing an outlet for the sale of produce
across the UK.

www.poultrypark.com 01989 721 066
www.hens4homes.co.uk 01371 878 909
www.forsham.com 01233 820 229
www.omlet.co.uk 0845 4502 056

All the above specialise in catering for the chicken keeper with
everything from poultry houses to courses.

The Good Life Press Ltd.
P O Box 536
Preston
PR2 9ZY
01772 652693

The Good Life Press publishes a wide range of titles for the smallholder, farmer and country dweller as well as **Home Farmer**, the monthly magazine for anyone who wants to grab a slice of the good life whether they live in the country or the city.

Other titles of interest:

A Guide to Traditional Pig Keeping by Carol Harris
An Introduction to Keeping Sheep by J. Upton/D. Soden
Build It! by Joe Jacobs
Build It ..with Pallets by Joe Jacobs
Craft Cider Making by Andrew Lea
Flowerpot Farming by Jayne Neville
Grow and Cook by Brian Tucker
How to Butcher Livestock and Game by Paul Peacock
Making Country Wines, Ales and Cordials by Brian Tucker
Making Jams and Preserves by Diana Sutton
The Bread and Butter Book by Diana Sutton
The Cheese Making Book By Paul Peacock
The Frugal Life By Piper Terrett
The Pocket Guide to Wild Food by Paul Peacock
The Polytunnel Companion by Jayne Neville
The Sausage Book by Paul Peacock
Showing Sheep by Sue Kendrick
The Smoking and Curing Book by Paul Peacock
The Urban Farmer's Handbook by Paul Peacock

www.goodlifepress.co.uk
www.homefarmer.co.uk

HomeFarmer *for dreamers and realists*

Home Farmer is the monthly magazine for anybody who wants to grab a slice of 'the good life' whether they live in the city or the country. Available through newsagents or by post

www.homefarmer.co.uk
visit us and become a fan on Facebook